walk… the…
in Wonder and Words

Letters from the Heart

Sharon Wakeford

First published by Sharon Wakeford, 2020

ISBN 978-0-620-89039-7(print)

Illustrations and cover drawing by Abigail Sligcher

Cover Design and Typesetting by Gregg Davies Media
(www.greggdavies.com)

CONTENTS

FOREWORD

Since the reanimation of the pilgrimage to Santiago de Compostela in Spain over forty years ago, hundreds of thousands of journals, blogs or vlogs have been written or screened by pilgrims describing their journeys on various Camino routes in Europe. Many have been turned into successful books or documentaries.

Walking The Way in Wonder and Words: Letters from the Heart differs from these in that the author has written a collection of letters to pilgrims and people she met on her 2019 Camino, or whom she carried with her from her previous Caminos. Seeing the extraordinary in the ordinary, describing places, people, and interactions in almost lyrical prose, each pilgrim or person, offers unique opportunities for her to practice what she has coined the *"L Words, words which hold equal measure of challenge and opportunity .... language, listening, loving, living, and learning."*

She shows that none of us is perfect and, even as an internationally accredited mediator and coach, she learns that the old maxim: *"When the student is ready, the teacher will appear"* is true. After an incorrect first impression of an Italian pilgrim she writes, *"and there on the terrace, the universe clearly had it in mind that this learner needed a teacher, to be reminded about the danger of ungrounded assessments, the untruths they tell, and the great disservice they do to both assessor, and those assessed."*

I recommend this book for all of life's learners. This is not a practical 'how to' walk the Camino. This collection of letters from 'The Way', is a 'how to' listen, love, and learn every day, not only on the Camino.

Sylvia Nilsen
Founder of 'amaWalkers Camino' and Camino author.
Durban, South Africa

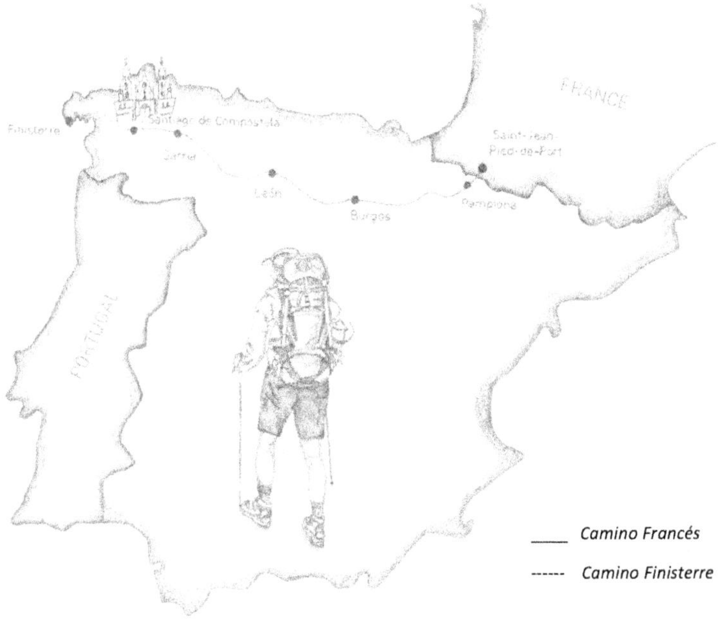
FRANCE
Finisterre
Santiago de Compostela
León
Burgos
Pamplona
Saint-Jean-
Pied-de-Port
PORTUGAL
Camino Francés
Camino Finisterre

Dear Sharon

I don't really know where to begin this letter or what exactly I want to say to you as you prepare once again, to set your feet onto the path, a path that crosses the expanses of Spain, as much as it runs like veins under your South African skin. Who would have thought that a passing conversation with a little known acquaintance in the small confines of an airless meeting room in downtown Johannesburg, could have provided the first fine threads for what would become the rich, multi-coloured, deeply-storied quilt that wraps so lovingly, and fiercely, around your heart and your identity?

With each year's path, more people, places, joys, sorrows, hopes, and yearnings have become woven into this quilt-of-your-heart. Some squares and circles carefully cut and seamlessly sewn, velvety to the touch, gently comforting to the soul. Others more random in their design and attachment – haphazard shapes, scratchy stitching that smoothed over the years, or didn't, and continues to prickle. Pieces more transient, that stayed for a few sleeps or seasons, and moulted away.

The quilt, as essential as your lightweight sleeping bag, now offers itself to you for a ninth time, in this year 2019. What new triangles and textures might be added I wonder? Any that might work their way loose or lose their colour or attraction? Stitches that feel smoother after their period of hibernation but become rough under the searing afternoon sun and temperamental Galician rain? Shapes and strands whose colours become sharper, more insistent – signalling their intention to step forward as teachers, or offer themselves as guides?

More obvious than the quilt, I observe your 'beloved' Deuter backpack, a descriptive term not usually extended to the inanimate, but in your case it feels right. The pack, with its cheerful, if somewhat weather-beaten yellow and blue flower attached to the one strap, and the sparkly yellow and blue ten centimetre figure of 'Solomon', who travelled a great many miles from Utah to accompany you to Spain. I see your agonised-over Black Diamond walking poles, your First Ascent zip-off walking pants, and your sole-moulded Salomon boots – all these invisible to the 'naked eye' off the path, but so embodied within your way of being. About to recover visibility. Ready to be of service on the practical path.

I wonder Sharon, who you would like to be in this beginning, of this year's path, and at this stage of your becoming? What could be different about you from the previous time, or the one before that, or even before that? Beyond the two new items that are joining the regular residents of your backpack – the new gleaming red Swiss Army knife, and the roll of packaging tape for your experimental rainproof boot coverings – what, do you hope to carry in your being? To what do you want to give home to on this path?

I notice something new in your hand, possibly part of a new becoming, an emergence, and I am curious about this, as you start your steps. The fingers of your left hand that close with such ease and efficiency around your walking pole, have increasingly been wrapping themselves, with joy and wonder, around the pale green stem of your already precious Lamy. A meaningful and meaning-filled gift to you from a dear friend, on your recent milestone birthday. An invitation to capture the 'here and now', but equally to dip its nib into an older, deeper, and more storied part of yourself.

What might grow from this fertile stem? Might there be fewer kilometres walked, and more worlds wandered in the words? What might that bring to the sights, sounds, and quality of the experience? You have always been a listener to others on your pilgrim paths, listening with your coach's curiosity, a listening, seductive to others. What horizons of possibility might listening into the silence, into the unspoken bring? Listening for the mysterious, and the mystical, for what might be given life to on or between the feint Irish lines of your notebook? And what reminder might the thin strands of white beads on your writing wrist bring – the Sangoma beads from Lwandle, a small reflection of her Sangoma journey – that sit as close to your heart as they do to your sun-browned skin, and that enable you to carry a small, yet significant, snippet of Africa with you as you journey in Europe?

I wish you a safe, blessed, and whole-being path – long or short, rough or smooth, scarce or abundant. Even more so, I wish you a path of deep presence, and a great many pauses.

Buen Camino.

Love

Sharon

Dear Jorge

A name I have no idea is yours, but one that I am choosing to call you. 'Farmer' or 'earth-worker' Google tells me is its meaning. You do not have fields or cattle, or maybe you do, I would not actually know, since I met you behind the counter of a café-bar, in what is not quite a village, but a few dull grey squares of houses, and a children's play area, forlorn and abandoned in the heat and stillness of the siesta. The bar, like its surrounds, unprepossessing, and seemingly with little to offer.

Not the lush greens of the Galician hills, or the attractive vines of the del Beirzo, but the dusty brown flatness of the recently harvested wheat fields, that creep around the bar and give it a place to be, to offer itself quietly and unpretentiously to a scattering of locals, and the passing tide of pilgrims, happy to be beyond the unforgiving asphalt and industrial sprawl, that is the leaving of León. The faded green chair that held my gratefully seated body, and the fine coating of dusk that brushed my forearms as I brought them to rest on the sun-scratched tabletop, were part of this gentle invitation to pause, before walking the barren brown road to Villar de Mazarife.

Despite my actual walked distance being only about a kilometre, I arrived at your bar with the weariness of a day's stage already in my shoulders and feet, and a lingering bitter taste in my mouth and mood. A day that had begun at 4h15 – an ungodly hour to wake, but a merciful release from the thin sleep – the only possible sleep allowed by the thumping of Madrid's Horteleza district. The early morning bus, a welcome quiet contrast, but four long hours of cold, bumpy discomfort on the journey north. The brilliant sunrise, an ineffectual heater against the staunch commitment of the air conditioner. The bus's empty back row, that held a promise of sleep, a promise sadly undermined by the raised cushioning and safety belt sockets that punctuated the row of adjoining seats.

León eventually. My hands, feet, and mood began to thaw as I made my way from the bus station towards the *centro de cuidad*. Although I would start walking a short bus ride out of León, I felt called to first stand under the majestic spires of the cathedral – to bless the space between an ending and a beginning – the ending of my 2017 Camino, and the beginning of this one. To open my arms and my heart, to whatever this year's path might offer or ask. To inhale deeply into possibility, mystery, and more challengingly, the unknown.

It would still be a couple of hours, a few hundred more city steps, and a stop in a different bar, before I would meet you, Jorge. The bar that accounted for the bitter taste that soured the 'official start' of this ninth Camino, and with whose residue I arrived at your bar counter, further along the path. Why the bitter taste you might wonder? It wasn't just the sharpness of the coffee, the unfriendliness of the café-bar owner, and the insistence of his *logica* in charging me, almost as much for the cups of hot water that I asked to accompany my espresso, as for the coffee itself. No, it was the taste of the crushing disappointment of how my journey was beginning. How lovely I had thought it would be to write my way into walking; to 'pause with pen' before starting my first stage. But where I had hoped for a smooth easing into, I got a rough scouring of steel wool.

Pen poised and espresso poured, I sat at the gleaming white table under the crisp white wooden umbrella in the small square of La Virgen del Camino, a small village seven kilometres beyond León. Seemingly set up. A slow midday exhale, after an arduous morning. Bam! The assault of loud phlegmy coughing. Involuntarily, I held my breath, waiting for an inevitable landing. And land it did, from upon high. I wanted, yet did not want, to trace its origin. A quick glimpse upwards across the square. A slender tattooed torso of a forty-something man, and not the anticipated potbelly of a seventy-plus someone. A brief ceasefire, and then another round of the hacking cough. The next landing awaited. Chinese water torture. I moved inside. Counterintuitive on such a glorious day; into the chill of the air conditioning, and a different array of auditory annoyances. Irritating to my sleep-deprived self, but less visceral than those outside.

So, how grateful I was Jorge, for so many things about your bar – that it sits quietly alone, not surrounded by life and limb or balconies from which projectiles might land. Grateful for its weather-beaten green chairs, and lightly dusted tabletops, so welcome and forgiving, after the glare of the pristine white outside-tables and posh dark wooden inside-tables at the Virgen café-bar, tables that dared you to mess on them. Grateful that there was no hungry machine with its repetitive carnival-like tune and intermittent clicks and dings. No one standing behind it, rattling *monetas* in their pocket, coins soon to be swallowed and possibly spat out, depending on the whim of the machine.

So grateful for the salty crunchiness on my tongue of the *papas fritas* that I bought from you, some eaten unaccompanied, one at a time, others in handfuls, crushed between the cheese and butter of the baguette that I had been waiting not-so-patiently to eat. Bread and cheese that I could never have bitten into in the Virgen bar, but that I could now freely wrap my fingers around. How I savoured every mouthful, for its own sake, and for its blotting out of the last traces of the earlier bitterness.

Down-at-heel. The way some might describe your bar, but I felt gently held by its ease and acceptance. A feeling of familiarity. I loved its whisper of "take me as I am", and its platoon of plants in their unregimented pots, dishes, and jars, intentionally or unintentionally formed into a display on the one outside wall. Plants and pots that took me back to the balcony of my great granny's flat above my father's shop. There, plants whose juicy leaves tumbled and tangled like thick green dreadlocks from their pots, and over their dusty saucers, which kept quiet company as my granny peeled her way through bag after bag of pickling onions. Where each onion was carefully, and efficiently, stripped of its papery skin, and had a small cross cut into its top, before it landed in the plastic basin of vinegar, peppercorns, mustard seeds, and bay leaves. A temporary resting place, before it continued its journey into the Consol jar, and onward to the customer, bringing a few much needed Rands to the family purse.

My great granny Hilda, not someone that I would have expected to encounter at a remote café-bar in a country she had never had the means to see. A country that, given her wholeheartedness, volume and volatility, would have resonated strongly with her. A woman who, like your bar, never pretended to be something she wasn't. A woman with so little to give, but who gave so much from her vinegar-wrinkled fingers and fiercely generous heart.

I thank you Jorge, for all your bar offered me, in the same wholly unassuming way my great granny offered so much to all in my family. Thank-you for the surprise of connecting her to me, and to my journey. But certainly my biggest appreciation was for answering 'yes' to the question I posed to you before leaving – could I take a photo of you and your friend as you smoked a cigarette under the pot plants? Because as I told you, I wanted to capture the essence and warm embrace of your café-bar in that moment, and your essence was essential to it. Not only did you beam consent with your whole being, but your theatrical gesture of rearranging all of the five hairs that sparsely populated your head, set me onto the hot, hard 17 kilometre path to Mazarife with a laugh on my lips and a lightness in my legs.

Thank-you for being an accidental farmer, for what you supported to grow in me, in my short time in your peaceful patch.

Saludos

Sharon

Hola David

I wonder where this letter finds your dancing dark eyes, and mischievous grin, your warm and engaging Spanish self? How it finds you in your great many questions, in your quest for finding solutions to the questions you were carrying in your Quechua backpack? The backpack you had bought just two days before stepping onto this path, the same day on which you were told that your employment contract would not be renewed, effectively rendering you unemployed a few short hours later. A rapid ending, and an equally hasty entry into the next thing – the Camino. No surprise that you were walking in running togs – the fresh black lightweight shorts and marathon-ready running shoes. A man trying to get somewhere quickly – to Santiago, as much as to a solution. 'Solution' implies a problem, and the problem gnawing at you, the problem that you wanted this Camino to solve – were you correctly in the profession of being an engineer, was this your true calling – and if not, what was?

But let me slow down to my pace, and not be moving at yours, not already be in the place of our conversation. Let me go back a few steps, a few hours, and locate you more carefully in my day. A day sparse in colour, connection, and conversation, before I met you in the courtyard of the beautiful Albergue San Miguel, as the sun was setting on the day. The albergue, a sanctuary of colour and canvases, of art and heart, a stone's throw from the ancient cobblestone bridge of Hospital de Orbigo. A bridge I gratefully crossed, after a modest but wearying walk from Villar de Mazarife. A bridge over the gargling-green of the Rio Orbigo, so welcome after the long swathes of thirsty brown flatness of the wheat fields, cut with the closeness of a barber's electric razor, with the odd spike poking upwards, like random hairs that eluded the humming shaver. Occasional struggling sunflowers, bottlebrushes among flecks of green, and postage stamps of small yellow and blue flowers, a few interruptions of colour, along the day's sparse, silent path.

The pace and pitch of the water beneath the bridge, not just music to my ears after the absence of tune and tone, but alive, and energetic. Pulling the moss into heads of fine green flowing hair. Heads feeling the freedom of the fast-moving water, and wanting to catch its downstream flow, but bodies held back, wrapped around rocks, trapped in the tight crevasses. The 'heads' like you David, you with your urgency to be moving on a fast-flowing stream to a 'solution'– to clarity, to identify your calling, a new direction.

But this is not what the Camino gives us. Never a path to swiftly or reliably satisfy one's more obvious desires. Never a speedy arrival at a hoped-for destination. Instead, a consistent stretching towards a surrender, a letting go, before any meaningful arrival is possible.

How long and arduous were my own early morning kilometres on the day I met you. A gloriously spacious, and salubrious sunrise. No thumper-thumper of a Madrid nightclub, no drunken revellers stumbling their way home, no crunching stickiness of boots on broken beer bottles, but rather the clean, quiet asphalt of the road out of the slumbering Villar de Mazarife. But soon, the straight stripe of tar became hard under my dusty Salomons, under the wait and weight of my yearning for coffee. Six kilometres my anticipation, but the satisfaction of my coffee craving was only to come after a torturous ten. Nothing quick about this, but rather a trudging, solitary, slowness.

Eventually an oasis. Tables and chairs alongside the deserted Saturday morning street in Villavante. The potential of attending to my empty tank, nutritionally and conversationally. My shoulders breathed as I peeled off my backpack. I became taller and lighter, lighter still, as I saw the large *napolitana* offering itself on the bar counter. The pastry puffed up, self-important, the hard chocolate plugging each end. An offer impossible to refuse. Placed on the table outside, as neighbour to a brightly coloured espresso cup, I took a moment to savour this marvellous specimen, to sniff deeply into its chocolatey invitation. But oh, the deflation of my first bite, the *napolitana* like a punctured tyre, lost its form and substance. The escaping air, however, inaudible over the sudden faceless voices circling around me. A moment's disorientation, as I tried to find the faces. The clue, the over-dramatic intonations and canned mood music – a 'soapie', by any language, is still a 'soapie'. This one was coming from the phone of a woman sitting two tables away, the 'soapie' buzzing mosquito-like around my head. Just be in the coffee I told myself. 'Block it out', as Dearly Beloved was always telling me. Not easy for someone with my acute hearing, and being somewhere 'on the spectrum' of misophonia.

The coffee slid down like an Olympic skier on the smooth steep descent of a ski jump. My feet luxuriously un-socked, outstretched on the plastic chair. How I wished in the slow savouring, for the 'soapie' to speed by, but it too, like so much else on this path, had to take its own not-so-sweet time. Then, a few short words for me with a man who joined the woman. The woman now poking at her phone, the 'soapie' mercifully, rinsed away. My conversation with him as short as his walk, just a single day of walking he said, preparing for later. A quick coffee for him. The growl of the black diesel Audi A6, and they were gone.

Rebooted, I stepped back onto the grey concrete, and towards a small gathering. Walking stick met bicycle. 'Andy cap' met peak cap, met sun hat. The gathering of six villagers and hundreds of words. A study in being slow, of taking time, of connecting about the minutiae of village life. A conversation that I was not part of, but that gently lapped at my boots.

Very different to the later dialogue with you David, that came in wave after wave of questions, some spaced and neatly formed, others haphazard and hurriedly chasing the one before it, like the south-easter's white horses galloping and breaking untidily onto Muizenburg beach.

Another thought, another question, another wave you washed on me. "Where did you start your Camino? Why do you walk the Camino? What do you do? Should I stick with being an engineer or find something else? Is this my calling? As a coach, Sharon, surely you can give me a solution?"

Your questions, seemingly far more appetising to you than the vacuum-packed egg and potato *tortilla* – a dense yellow frisbee, not going anywhere. You got your fork into it, but never your heart or your teeth. I, on the other hand, relishing the mouthfuls of fried mushrooms, onions, red peppers, and eggs, and a heavy shower of Parmesan-style cheese. Wallowing in the deliciousness of the soft centred baguette with butter and *queso curado*. A long-awaited dinner, simple, yet wonderfully abundant, a sharp contrast to the morning's 'pretender pastry'.

A smooth spoonful of tasty peach yoghurt on my tongue, another question on your lips.

"Are Spanish men more driven to success and more emotional than other men, and less likely to show vulnerability?"

A question you asked after you learned that I was coaching two Spanish men.

"Isn't it dangerous to show vulnerability, won't it just be seen as weakness?"

I peeled open the plastic of another *yogur melacoton*, another question.

"Do you believe in science or God, Sharon?"

How much your thirty-year-old self and way of being reminded me of another thirty-year-old I had worked with, – a coaching client, Muhammad. A young man a continent away from you, but like you, with an insatiable curiosity and questioning; a man who described himself to me as having a splinter in his brain – something that would jab at him until he found an answer to whatever question he was sitting with.

I drifted to my South African shores, and more deeply into my remembering of Muhammed, when your next question, a very different one, sprayed on my face.

"Being 50, Sharon, can you walk 30 kilometres a day?"

A light drizzle landed a spit and a spot on my sun-browned arms. The universe gently inserting itself into the conversation, saying "Pause a moment, be still, look around, notice what is beyond this Q&A."

Guitar strumming drifted into the courtyard. A group of around fifteen Italians having some kind of mass in the albergue's lounge area. An invitation had earlier been offered to me to join them, but I declined, preferring to cook my dinner and enjoy the quiet of the courtyard, and the evening sun's gentle back massage. A quiet, that would certainly be overtaken, once the Sicilians began their supper.

A quiet day it was, David, until we washed up at the same supper table, and indeed my conversation tank, that had begun the day with a shallow coating from the night before, and had run dry over the kilometres to

Hospital de Orbigo, was now filled to overflowing, through the time and tides of our being together.

Full up, it was time to take my leave of the intensity of your curiosity and questioning David, and to listen into the voices of the village. To the whisper of the leaves on the tall trees standing in formation alongside the river, to the exuberance of the locals with their *vino tinto* and *tapas*, to the children playing soccer on the field alongside the caravan park. To step into the unexplored sights and streets of the village, with gratitude to you for the warmth and wonder of the connection, and an appreciation for the stillness in the space beyond it.

And in that stillness, I swam soundlessly in your captivating question about age and distance. Such a gift to be given this question at this stage of my journey, only one day in. A question that I answered in a heartbeat, not with a statement, but rather, with a question of my own. "Would I want to?" A question, whose answer I would live into, for the nearly four hundred kilometres and seventeen days the path offered ahead of me.

And for your path ahead David, was my hope that you would be able to walk this way of St James in the company of your questions. To be a patient, and curious listener to those questions that had already expressed themselves, and to allow space and invitation for those still to be born. To loosen the straps on your need for solutions. To listen into the silence, and the whispering of the wind, because who knows what call they could carry?

Warm regards

Sharon

B*onjour* David

A new day, a new David. After my hours of evening intensity with Spanish David, how wonderful it was to walk in the ease and spaciousness of the early afternoon connection, with you and your delightful sons. My own experience of *liberté, égalité,* and *fraternité,* and an observation of 'democracy in action'.

My first sighting of you, David, and your *fils,* was from a distance, a picture of paradox. In a single frame, your three young sons – the symmetry of black shorts, walking sticks, loose limbs growing taller with each fluid Spanish step – and an old Castilian village woman in her floral dress, and bright turquoise house slippers, shoulders rounded, shrinking with each advancing year, and slow step up the hill into the tiny village of Santibáñez *de* Valdeiglesia.

Just ahead of her, a crocheted beige cap with red and white stripes, a peeping periscope over your broad backpack. Not your typical Camino hat, but accompanied by your three sons, neither were you, David, a typical *peregrino*. A pilgrim my curiosity called me to walk alongside, but whose invitation into conversation or even less so, connection, I could not be sure of.

An invitation that did come, just after this sighting, was a different invitation – to pause with pen and coffee, in this delightful village, at a café-bar at the top of the hill. To be tucked into a glorious square of sunlight, and be in the yin and yang of the sweet lemony tang of a *magdalena*, something between muffin and cupcake, and the dark roasted coffee beans, awash in the smooth jazzy strains of Eve St Jones' '*Blaming it on the Boogie*'.

The sudden interruption to my hand's flow over the polished pine table and Eve's melodious musings, an ungodly racket, that on closer listening proved to be a 'Godly noise'. Sunday mass being bellowed from above. Not directly from the 'One' above, but through two giant speakers, standing sentry, on each side of the church bell on its tall steeple. Speakers as sturdy as Beefeaters, but anything but silent or circumspect, standing solid on a place more typically occupied by the storks.

In my surveillance for the source, head up from my book, eyes scanning, into view came three glasses of orange juice at a table towards the bar. Sun-browned skinny arms of early teenagers. My ears strained against the deafening mass, and in the respite between singing and sermon, the light dancing voices, and English words dripping heavy French accents, like croutons dunked in a thick onion soup. Your boys, David, speaking to fellow pilgrims in the bar. Your boys back in my line of sight. A possibility of conversation, a chance to quench my curiosity? No, not yet. My break with coffee and cursive had already been quite lengthy, and my nerves were nearing their threshold of tolerance for the barking Beefeaters. It was time for me to move on. Besides, would engaging in conversation against the overwhelm of the Sunday service, not have been doing this gentle art a disservice?

The mass still ringing in my ears, I hobbled my discombobulated self, back onto the path, and with each step, a receding of the noisy tide and a re-centering, onwards and upwards into the hills beyond Santibáñez. Quiet, except for the rhythmic crunching of my Salomons on the neat gravel road, the subtle hiss of a bicycle tyre, a chuckle in my throat as I caught sight of 'Pluto' – splayed body, floppy ears and pink tongue, atop a pannier bag progressing up a long hill towards Astorga. On this path, pilgrims in all shapes and sizes, forms and furs.

Smooth became rough, bumpy gravel ups, and sandy, stony, downs, until a long ascent spat me out of the forest and onto a dry, bald expanse of scrubby flat land. Bald, except for the pilgrim oasis. Not the red or white tables and chairs, or green umbrellas of a café-bar, but a ramshackle collection of faded multicoloured cloths unkindly treated by the sun's harsh stare. Couches and cushions, jaded by the support given to weary life and limb, and mismatched tree-stump seats and tables. The so-called 'Pilgrim House', and a pause in the liminal kilometres between Santibáñez and Astorga.

While I appreciated the incredible goodwill of the skinny long-haired host, and his abundant *donativo* offerings of healthy edibles, for me, just a freckled, sweet-smelling golden apple. However, its promise of deliciousness unfulfilled, instead, a floury tastelessness.

But deliciousness came, David, shortly after I dumped my mouse-nibbled apple, when I caught up with you and your boys, in the wide still flatness of the path, just beyond the Pilgrim House. An opportunity at last, to give voice to my many musings about your family foursome. But before I could proceed on the conversational path alongside you, a question of permission, because certainly, so much of my curiosity would already have been the subject of others' questions. Questions like my floury apple, for which you might no longer have an appetite to answer. A cheerful *oui* and a smile that crinkled out from under the crocheted hat, when I asked if I could ask you a few things, and so it was, that four became five, as we made our way over as many richly conversationed kilometres to Astorga.

How I loved being a listener to the story of you and your boys, your 13-year-old twins and your young 10-year-old, of your walking the 800 kilometre path from Saint Jean Pied de Port to Santiago, of previous walks when the boys were ten and seven, of the inspiration you were to the many parents you met along the path, parents who began to see possibilities opening for them and their own children. David, to be not just in the sweetness of my listening, but also in the fullness of my observation, of observing your way of being with your boys, your ways of doing. To see how each of you walked at your own pace, sometimes alongside each other, sometimes at intervals like roped Himalayan climbers. No rope required here, so strong was the thread of deep, loving, and respectful connection between you four on the path, and a longer thread to your wife, at home in Avignon, who would join your line in a few weeks' time in Santiago.

But you, Emil, Etienne, and Pierre, did not just travel as a line, but also a circle. A circle in which all voices and views were heard, in which decisions were made. How far you would walk, when you would break, where you would stay, decisions not made from under the crocheted hat, but through discussion and collective engagement. Walking the talk of democracy. So, for me, David, even more inspiring than your doing of the 800 kilometres, your way of being, as a parent on this path.

How much I loved dipping into a different chapter of this French narrative, into the story of you. Like the Spanish David I had met the day before, you too had come to a point in your life where you had questioned whether your profession was your vocation, your two decades of being an 'informatician'. A place of security and certainty, but also a place of confinement and limitation, building formulas and models on the small, smooth, lifeless surface of a keyboard. Whereas, the call of your hands and heart, was to large, rough, life-giving stone. To build, and shape, to feel form and substance under artisanal fingers. And so, with your desire in your hands, and the courage in your heart, you chipped your way through a year's apprenticeship as a stonemason, and for the past 10 years had been in the passion and creativity of your true calling. This individual journey, as inspiring as the collective one with your sons.

And beyond your stories and my observations, David, what a joy it was to be wonderfully in the flow and expansiveness of conversation with you. So different to the clear channels of enquiry with young Spanish David, our conversation, a rich mangrove forest with a multitude of passageways to be ventured into. Walking, callings, conflict, coaching, Mitterrand, Mandela, relationships, Ramaphosa, Macron, marriage, meaning, purpose, being, and becoming. A venturing without sequence, or linearity, but with glorious *liberté.*

How often on the Camino, David, my conversations default into coaching ones, where the scales weigh heavily towards myself as listener, poser of questions, be they curious or powerful, inviting of reflection and self-exploration. A default that I had cautioned myself about before starting this year's path. Not to slip into being a 'Camino coach', but to be an equally 'air-timed' conversation partner, or just to be in the sweet territory of silence. My time with you, David, with your questions and curiosity, the attentiveness of your listening, left this box not just ticked, but fully plastered. Blessed *égalité.*

And between meanderings and musings, companionable silences. One silence into which strong strumming inserted itself. Three chords and the belting out of three words "oh, oh *peregrino*", a guitar spun and slapped by a flat hand in the small of its weather-beaten back, while the other hand pointed at a cap with coins.

Your coins clinked, on we continued. Kilometres through the outskirts of Astorga, ones that in previous years had been hard and long, now glided underfoot. Even the scorpion's tail, the final stinging uphill into the *centro*, lost its poison in the smoothness of our stories and silences. Energy and breath that still remained as we took our last few steps together into Astorga. Steps of a shared purpose, but more so, a brief, yet beautiful sharing of friendship on this journey, and of our life's journeys. A gift of *fraternité*.

I would not see you or your sons again along this path, but I knew, David, that after you finished this Camino you would be starting another. One that like this one, would be steeped and stepped in paradox. Because, before setting foot on this path, after years of being self-employed, and being within the abundance of your family in Avignon, you had landed your "dream job" with a company to restore a city full of antiquities. An offer that must have made your fingertips tingle, but the acceptance of which, would take you on a path to Nice, away from your beloved wife and sons, for the first nine months at least. A path with many uncertainties. A path of heart and hope, of highs and lows, of gifts and challenges. A path different, yet so similar to the one upon which we met.

Bonne chance, David, and for the blessedness of our walk, *merci beaucoup.*

Warmly

Sharon

C*iao* Marciela

Soft hands. Plump and browned. Hands that held mine at the bottom of the seven stone steps that joined the cool, leafy sanctuary of La Posada's downstairs *terraza,* to its busy street-level bar. A tiny green lung that, for the most part, held just three of us in its gentle breathing embrace, you, your dear Dorian, and me. Nourished, and nurtured, away from both the hot hills, and the fierce air conditioning of the bar above.

Getting to know you, Marciela, did not happen in a conventional Camino way. No synchronisation of steps and sticks along the path, no café-bar coffee conversation. The route to knowing you was somewhat different, a matter for my senses and sensibilities. Senses called forth in a different order, led by sound, and later followed by sight and touch. A journey through my sensibilities from a place of assumption and judgement, albeit subtle, through acceptance to appreciation.

And so, to our meeting.

Chairs scraped lightly on the concrete floor. A disturbance to the tranquillity of the terrace, to the ease and solitude, so welcome, after the high 'amps' of Constance, my last hour's walking partner. You and your companion were seated by the host-cum-server, at the centre of the terrace, at the centre of his attention. A lively exchange between you and him, that pushed Coldplay into the terrace's furthest corners. Spanish, Italian, Spanish, Italian, a coin being flipped again and again. The host's Spanish tones low, lightness and laughter bubbling in your higher Italian pitch. Excitement and enthusiasm as you surveyed the menu, made your selection. A process, not a single action. A *plato primero* penned on the host's pad, but then an excited exclamation, a dish more enticing. The selection scratched out, and replaced by another, then another, then on to your *plato segundo*, a similar process of enthusiastic discovery. Eventually, your three courses on paper, the quiet, decisive, one-time delivery of your companion's order.

The host retreated, a moment of silence. Coldplay's *'Yellow'* came back into play, now accompanied by humming, the tune easy for your companion's lips, the words I assumed, foreign to his tongue. A harmless assumption on my part, but one in a series that was to follow. A quick sideways peek at you and him. "It's rude to stare, Sharon", my mother's decades' ingrained words. Fresh faces, clean clothes, feet sandaled, not booted. All this, at only 12h30. Too early to be this clean and shiny, to be this chipper, too early to have already walked a day's stage. Pilgrims? No, my assessment declared. Day visitors, Astorga's cathedrals and plazas explored, some sightseeing into the countryside, and lunch in the beautiful village of Rabanal del Camino.

A sudden dramatic interruption to the story I was so carefully crafting, and to your companion's cheerful humming. High volume, a high voltage attack on my nervous system. What the hell? My head jolted upwards. Momentarily, a remote control in my line of sight before it withdrew and dropped to the host's side like a cowboy's smoking Colt. Spanish TV blasted into the *terraza,* a cruel assault on this quiet, contented place.

You might remember, Marciela, my clumsy Spanish plea.

"Por favor, es possible no tener el television? Es muy tranquilo antes del televisiòn".

The three of us stared at the host, awaiting his next move. Would he blink, our John Wayne of Rabanal? No, his look, somewhere between blank and frown. No rapid movement, no movement at all. We waited in suspense. Slowly his hand rose. Aim, fire, the TV was shot down.

"Es okay para ti?" I asked you, somewhat after the fact.

"Si" you replied, your wide mouth and light eyes smiling their complete agreement. With marching arms and stamping feet, you communicated to the host that after the miles of movement and noise, the quiet of the terrace was what was yearned for. The briefest nod he gave you.

"Como una funeria" his muttering, as he skulked up the stone stairs, away from the 'funeral-like' terrace.

Calm restored, you returned to your conversation with your companion, and I picked up my pen. All quiet, except for the gentle rhythmic sound of a big knife cutting large arches, on a wooden board in the kitchen adjoining the terrace. But the external calm and quiet gave way to the prickling, poking discomfort of my questions – questions about the story that I had been telling myself about you and your companion. The tourist story, tourists, whom my story deemed had not actually earned a three- course lunch. The story that your swinging arms and stamping feet had so decisively declared untrue.

My frown lines pinched tightly on my forehead, a churning in my gut. Guilty. Guilty of making an ungrounded assessment about you and your companion, an assessment that carried with it the subtle judgment of 'less earned, less than'. But you two were oblivious to my discomfort and disquiet, as the clatter of crockery and cutlery, and giant silver bowl, signalled the landing of your *platos primeros*.

You sat forward, and I sat back, took another swallow of my tea. Despite my fundamental belief that there was no 'right way' to do the Camino, and that every persons' way was their way to be moulded into whatever shape or form worked for them – how far, how fast, for how long they chose to walk – there on the terrace, I had not even ventured into that space, no other possibilities contemplated, so sure was I of the 'truth' of my version. Yet you and your lunch mate were not tourists, but were indeed on the pilgrim path, on the very same path as me, maybe just with a slightly different rhythm and routine. How different the eyes through which we saw each other? Yours, kind, welcoming brown pools. Mine, clear blue, narrowed by the story I'd scripted, a story now, an indigestion in my stomach.

"Bon appetite" I wished you, and was rewarded with another of your broad smiles, just the edges visible on each side of the big round soup spoon.

"La sopa es molto bene" your half Spanish, half Italian response.

"Muy bien" I returned your infectious grin. The start of a more real connection, an exchange of short lines and smiles, between sips and swallows.

Your lunch eaten and my cups of tea drunk, we advanced to second base. Actual conversation, or conversation such as both our Spanish allowed, at the bottom of the big stone steps, as you and your companion prepared to head to your lodgings, and I, to rejoin the path to Foncebadón. A conversation more felt than spoken, in which I discovered the softness of your hands, the embrace of your energy. Learned the name by which you are called, Marciela. Marciela, originally from Romania, but long-time resident in Modena in northern Italy. Marciela, wife of Dorian, the still waters to your babbling brook.

I left with my thin fingers feeling the imprint of your soft fleshy hands, hands that I was not surprised to hear comforted and cared for so many at the hospitals of Modena. I left, Marciela, with laughter in my heart. Laughter that bubbled up from the strangest source – *'allora'*. A word that I told you was one of the few Italian words I knew. I word I did not use myself, but an ever-present word that preceded or peppered so many Italian sentences. A word that said little, but bought time – 'So', 'then', 'well'.

"Allora" I rolled the word off my tongue again.

You grinned and shook your head. With arms rolling and a circus ringmaster's bend, you laughed a loud *allora*. Clearly a word not just to be verbalised, but fully embodied. And so, with a final chorused, arm rolling *allora*, off we went, on our respective ways and into the not knowing of whether there would be any more *alloras*.

As I trod the hot, sandy, and unpilgrimed afternoon path to Foncebadón, my thoughts, Marciela, meandered to another *allora*, to another set of unserving, unkind assessments. To Italian Giorgia, a director at an international organisation in Rome to whom I consult. A woman of compassion, commitment, and wholeheartedness, whose sentences were generously *'allora'd'*. A woman, therefore, not dissimilar to you, and whom I had similarly subjected to assumption and judgment on our first meeting. A meeting when she attended mediator skills training I had developed, and was piloting, with a sample group of Legal and HR staff from her organisation. A training she participated in with varying attendance and attention. Participation that I assumed to reflect her lack of interest or commitment. But, like with you, Marciela, a woman I had to 're-story' when I was able to see and feel more deeply into her world. When it became clear that *my* story of her was not *the* story of her, that she was not inattentive or uncommitted, but juggling with great care, huge handfuls of organisational complexity and conflict, handfuls that would have made most in her position flatly refuse the request to attend the training. A slower journey with Giorgia into understanding and appreciation, far slower than my journey with you, Marciela, there on the *terraza*. But both journeys that ultimately brought large helpings of heart and humanness, and a joyful appreciation for all the *alloras*.

How happy I was, Marciela, to be blessed along the way with a few more *alloras*, that came as warm and welcome as a hot toddy, magically, on cold stretches of path. What a joy, many days after our terrace connection, on the biting, blustery climb to O Cebreiro, to unexpectedly spot you and Dorian ahead of me. To hear your great big laugh as I bellowed *allora* from behind you. To be greeted by your wide smile, and dancing brown eyes. Even more so, to be metaphorically spun around by your rolling barrel arms and sweeping bow, and to be swallowed up by your booming *allora* that responded to mine.

A grateful connection it was for me, Marciela, one that carried me up the long, cold, kilometres to O Cebreiro, and continued to warm me along the chilly windswept way to Fonfría. But beyond the gift of your warmth, my deep gratitude for your accidental teacher. It is said that "when the learner is ready, the teacher arrives". And there on the terrace, the universe clearly had it in mind that this learner needed a teacher, to be reminded about the danger of ungrounded assessments, the untruths they tell, and the great disservice they do to both assessor, and assessed.

Thank you, Marciela, for accepting the universe's request and offering yourself to me on that day, and for traveling in my backpack for very many more.

Allora!

Sharon

Dearest Danielo

I wonder where this letter finds you, and how it finds you, along your post-Camino path? Our time together was short, an overlap of just 48 hours and 28 kilometres on the path between Murias de Rechivaldo and the Cruz de Ferro. Yet, a sense of our souls having travelled a far greater distance together, not just in length, but also in breadth and depth. For me at least, because I cannot know if you felt the companionship of my soul, as you made your slow way to Santiago, carrying your hurting hamstring, carrying a burden that my observer saw weighing so heavily upon you, that made you seem older than your thirty-seven years. A burden, whose form and content I would never know, and never needed to know, to walk alongside you on the path of life.

My first impression of you, Danielo, was one of careful containment. You, my upper bunk neighbour in the cool, dark, dorm room of the Albergue Las Aguadas, in the tiny Mogato village of Murias de Rechivaldo. A village that would not be an obvious overnight stop for most pilgrims, given its proximity to the bigger, brighter, busier, Astorga. Clearly, we were both drawn to the small square of window at the far end of the dormitory, a window that blessed with light, the space between us. On the one side of the window, your backpack, a smart, red, no-nonsense post box alongside your bunk, the contents of which were carefully contained, with nothing visible to the outside eye, except for your sleeping bag, a precise single stripe on your bunk, an equal distance from each corner of the mattress. My empty blue Deuter pack, slumped against my bunk, only just avoiding total collapse. My bunk, a sea of flotsam and jetsam, virtually the entire insides of my pack having been upended onto the smooth, white sheet, a proper bedsheet, not the crinkly paper one, often encountered, with its teasing, testing elasticated corners. Me, sweaty, dusty, badger-busy in my arriving, a rummaging routine of separating and sorting stuff, storing valuables. You, clean, quiet, slow rhythmic strokes up and down the back of your thigh. Surprisingly, no accompanying smell of eucalyptus, or perhaps, more a matter of its scent simply not being able to compete with the strength of my salty sweat.

Sorry, I smiled at you, a smile of empathy, a smile of knowing the pain of injury on this path – not just the physical pain, but the ache of unmet expectations, and emotions. No words, just a sad smile that you returned. So quiet you were, Danielo, that I thought you didn't speak English, that ours would be only a connection of eyes and energy, of understanding, given and received.

But no, words would come. Slowly. Carefully. Me, being deliberate to be measured in pace, because if I was, the space between us could hold not just light, but language. A space we ventured into in the glorious clear sunlight of Santa Catalina, one village along the pink and purple-hued morning path from Murias. What blessings my habit of lingering long over coffee brought, not just in the deliciousness of the savouring of each alternate mouthful of coffee and the chocolately *napolitana*, but without my long linger, the gift of our connection would never have been unwrapped.

The chair into which you seated yourself had just been vacated by a native English speaker, a New Yorker who had provided company for my first cup. A woman on a similar professional path, who brought an avalanche of words and thoughts, but a scarcity of presence – who unknowingly spoke to, but not with me. How ironic, Danielo, that you, of Italian tongue, and quiet way, would occupy the chair so differently. To allow my second cup to be swallowed in spaciousness, story, and being seen. To be woven together in the most delightfully surprising way, not just through the strands of this 'Way of St James', but on an entirely other track.

"Where in Rome do you live"? I asked.

"Jonio", your reply.

JONIO. Black lettering on a white background came back into view, a whooshing in my ears, as the capsule, like a big metallic pill, brought itself to a stop. The lettering, a guide to me of whether I was going in the right direction on Rome's Metro Line B – the line that runs between Laurentina and Jonio. Laurentina, home to one of my international consulting clients, home to Giorgia, and all her *alloras*.

"Do you know about Jonio?" you asked me.

I explained my geographical knowing – how Jonio helped to locate me. And now it located you, being home to you, your wife, and your work as a furniture salesman.

But how much more there was about Jonio than being the end of the line, and how wonderful to be in your telling of the story of Jonio. A place of historical significance – not simply as an entry point into one of the world's greatest ancient cities, but the point from which Rome was liberated by Allied Forces in June of 1944. A liberation that ended a long and difficult siege of people and place.

Listening into the silence after your story, and reading between the few short lines of you that you shared with me, I wondered, Danielo, what might have been besieging you? I had no data, no 'intel' from the front line, simply a deep sensing under my skin that a war was being fought within you, a war that weighed so heavily on your shoulders, beneath your outwardly orderly backpack. A war of many struggles and skirmishes, one of which had inflicted injury upon you, which slowed your advance to Santiago, but against which you soldiered bravely on. I wondered whether this Camino might offer itself as a possible path towards liberation. Perhaps, your own personal Jonio?

With stories told, and others untold, it was time for us to take leave of Santa Catalina, but not before some exchanges of practical information, such is the pilgrim way. Based on information that had been transmitted to you, you warned me against staying at the Druid albergue in Foncebadón, the village of my intended overnight stop. And I relayed to you, the name, Guacelmo, a delightful *refugio* in Rabanal, 10 kilometres away, a destination that your aching hamstring would allow you to reach. A place run by the kindly, if fussing, English *hospitaleros* associated with the Confraternity of St James, a place of a four o'clock community of tea and biscuits in the garden.

Information given and affirmatively received, and Jonio tucked gratefully in my pocket, we stepped our different paces onto the uphill path towards Rabanal. You, with the carefulness of the injured, and me, with a wondering of whether I would ever get to know more of the war I so strongly sensed you were silently engaged in, of the struggles that cast shadows on your step and smile. A question that might only be answered by the 'Camino Angels'.

And indeed, the angels obliged – not to answer my question, but to offer us another slice of time together. How sweet and soulful was our early morning connection the next day, in Foncebadón. The lightness of the crumbly, coconutty Santiago tart with its icing-sugar-moustaches, a contrast to the sadness that I felt seeping from your skin. A sadness, somehow infused with serenity, or was it maybe an exhaustion – the exhaustion of one who has struggled, wrestled for hours or days, and was still standing? Through red-rimmed eyes and slow speech, you told me about your time in Rabanal, your conversation with the Sicilian priest, a pilgrim-priest on the path with his group of fifteen whom I had met some days before at the beautiful Albergue San Miguel in Hospital de Orbigo. A priest, who had seen your pain, who prayed for you at Rabanal's pilgrim mass, who welcomed your tears. A welcome your still-red eyes signalled that you had completely surrendered to.

And all that your being asked of me, between my mouthfuls of coffee and cake, was to be a presence, a listener to your story. I did not need to know the words and ways of every chapter, of every line in the book of you, but just to gently hold a few paragraphs in my hands and heart. I thank you, Danielo, for entrusting this task to me, for allowing me to be your witness, for letting me into the sacredness of your struggle, and your vulnerability.

I would see you only one more time, just beyond the Cruz de Ferro, one of the most significant places along the entire *Camino Francés*. A place of pause, of reconnection to the purpose of the journey, to add a stone, or a token of love and blessing, to the place that witnesses our collective pilgrim journey. The place where you had stopped to pray, and where your prayers were so insensitively interrupted by two pilgrims, by their immediate need for a posing picture.

I do not know, Danielo, if, as you stepped your slow, cautious path to Santiago, you felt my hands holding your heart. I hope you did. I wonder if you could feel me smiling at you on the cliffs of Finisterre, where I took the final steps of my journey? Where I so unexpectedly came upon the Sicilian priest and his group of fifteen. Whether you felt me, as I offered them my heartfelt congratulations, and they offered me a laughing handful of their celebratory Santiago tart?

But more than my hope of any remembering, or feeling of me, Danielo, is my deeper yearning for you – that somewhere along the path to Santiago, or on the path beyond Santiago, that you found your way towards some lightness and liberation, or that it found its way to you. That your injury was not just a curse, but in the unfathomable way that is the way of the Camino, a gift – that a longer, slower, and more paused path, was what you needed, to live into your own Jonio.

May God be with you, wherever and however you are.

Sharon

Hello Sia

How wonderful your greeting. Delightful dimples that book-ended a wide smile. Dimples accompanied by a declaration, "I was coming to jump on your bed tonight!" In your hand, the rectangular wooden block with its carved '104'.

The key to my private room in the mountain hamlet of Foncebadón, a room I was prepared to pay for, after viewing several albergues that ranged from creepy, to airless, to soulless. The only place that really appealed to me, the Pension El Trasgu with its modern, clean brown brick, and sunny terrace, but alas, no rooms at that inn. And so it was, that I became the holder of room key 104 at another establishment. A key that I left on the counter of El Trasgu's *tienda*, so distracted were my thoughts, by the conversation with a Russian pilgrim, and my hands that were corralling the hard-crusted mahogany bread, tomato, boiled eggs, and yoghurt that would serve as my supper.

Damn! My discovery of 'keyless-ness' when I arrived at the door to 104, and back down the hill I went. My sweaty irritation, no match for the barrels of your Basque laughter, and the playfulness in your being, as you held the wooden block. How could I not laugh and meet your cheeky grin, with my own cheeky thought. That there are worse things that could happen, than an attractive, dark-haired woman, threatening to jump on your bed!

Like the 12th century hermit Gaucelmo, who gave refuge to pilgrims treading the treacherous, repenting path to Santiago, so too Sia, do you give refuge to the multitude of pilgrims along the modern-day path. Not dressings, bandages, and bowls of peasant soup, but heart, humour, and hugs, in the strange energy that is Foncebadón.

"Rabid dogs and an abandoned railway line" the main descriptors of many guidebooks. A once thriving high mountain village, that by the 1900s was home to just two residents living amongst its ruins. A village that in the early 2000s became a different kind of high, as the so-called hippies trickled in with their tents and tepees. People drawn to a different way of living, a different way of being. Although Sia, you were not part of this tide of dreadlocks and bright, billowing pants, you too were drawn to the call of the land, to make a different way from the world of your native San Sebastian, a world of the known, hundreds of kilometres to the north east.

Had you understood the demands of making a home in this fierce and unforgiving place, had you been ten years older, you simply would not have had the physical strength to meet the challenges that living this life required of you. To survive the harsh, biting winters, the suffocation of seven days of being snowed in, in the one room that was, at that time, the extent of the house that your hands had built. Not just physical, but emotional confinement. Struggles, that your stories told of a world 'out there' that tested every ounce of your being, as much as the internal war that dear Danielo was waging, was stretching and straining him.

I know for myself, even in the transience of the pilgrim path, the weight of heavy skies, and whipping wind, on my own internal weather pattern. Know too well the territory into which my mood would meander, or march, on days of limited connection and conversation. And this, with only my pilgrim's toes in the water. Not the deep dive into a declaration to build a life from nothing. No water, no electricity, no bricks and mortar. To build simply, or not so simply, from the foundation of your tremendous yearning.

And in your telling, to my mind came the wonderful words of Mary Oliver, to my interpretation of how this place was for you, Sia.

"A place that offered itself to your imagination

called to you like the wild geese – harsh and exciting

over and over announcing your place in the family of things."

And so it was, that you trod your own path, a path as treacherous as the medieval pilgrims' path, a path of learning and resilience, one foot in front of the other, towards competence in the practicalities of an off-the-grid life. To set up a water purification system, to plant, to grow, to know what you needed to know. A difficult process of learning, in the unconnected remoteness of the mountains. Weekly trips down the mountain, to Astorga, many miles away, to the library with its internet access, armed with your notebook, and your determination to build and create.

How different this world, the world of your story, from the one in which you and I would meet. The comforting cocoon of El Trasgu's bar and restaurant, the place of your summer labours. Gentle music, no interruption by Spanish television, just the intermittent hissing of the coffee machine. Smooth, brown floor tiles, giving way to peaceful, beige wall tiles, divided between floor and ceiling, by a line of small squares, of conch shells and lighthouses. Small squares that invited me, a lover of lighthouses, to pause. To be in the stillness that is a lighthouse, in the knowing of its role as guide, illuminating an onward journey, in the appreciation of its ability to stand steady, no matter the elements around it.

How wonderful it was, to pause on my onward path, in the warm welcome of this bar, to be in the wonder of your smile, and to feast on your story. How I loved learning your story, sentence by sentence. How I would have loved to have been able to sit down with you, to hear your story as one generous helping of pasta, rather than in the *tapas*-like servings – a taste of this, a sample of that, between the *cafes con leche, cafés solos* and *Americanos* you brought to life from the gleaming, steaming machine, between the frothy beers you pulled from the shiny silver tap. Pouring and pulling, that was your financial saviour you said, that supported you in sustaining the home to which you returned each night of the summer season, to the small family of your partner and two dogs, to 'your place in the family of things'.

And so, I returned to the café-bar, the morning after our previous afternoon's first meeting, when I had come to retrieve my key. I returned, not just to be once more, in the breadth of your smile and your story, but also to call you on your broken promise, on your failure to come and jump on my bed!

Your laughter, as warm as the coffee you placed before me, that I savoured each sip of, as I drunk in more of your telling. A telling and a connection that would fill my tank, a tank as important to be filled, as your rainwater one. A tank that would sustain my mood and movement on the day ahead. A tank now refilled, after the slow seepage of my silent night.

I had not minded the quiet of my private room, my single supper, eaten at the dressing-table-cum-dining-room-table, that I dragged under the window to gaze into the valley below. Certainly, I would have been grateful for some meeting of minds and meanings, as the sun withdrew her dimming rays from the day. But on my evening wandering, just a grubby handful of beer-soaked pilgrims whom I felt no desire to step towards, and a disinterested horse, who indulged my few sentences, as a light wave of alienation washed over me. A feeling of the abandoned Foncebadón of yesteryear. A feeling so 'other', now that I was with you.

So Sia, we did not jump on the bed, but I did bounce up and down in the ends of your wide smile, in the lightness of your laughter, in the sweetness of the Santiago tart that you served to Danielo and I, in the tranquillity of the morning terrace. I left the village with a joy in my heart, and a gratitude in my soul. Grateful for the richness and playfulness of our connection, for the gift that is a connection with one not directly on the pilgrim path. I also left with a great curiosity about what I might find along the way.

"There will be a surprise for you, Sharon, two kilometres after the iron cross", the words that followed your parting hug.

"A surprise for me?"

"Yes", you confirmed, "two kilometres after the cross".

And as my Salomons and sticks fell once more into step, I wondered, Sia, what if anything, I might have left you with? A sense of having been seen and heard a little more deeply, with possibly additional paragraphs of your story carried along the pilgrim path, and to lands far away? Of having been seen as more than the beguiling Basque barista, of being known as the woman whose hands had not just quenched the thirst and hunger of passing pilgrims, but whose hands had built a house and a life. A life that you so fully occupied in the beautiful desolation beyond Foncebadón. A house tucked into the folds of a hill two kilometres beyond the iron cross. A house that I passed with a lightness in my step, and a hug in my heart, and the question of what surprise I might find, answered.

With love, gratitude, and warm wishes

Sharon

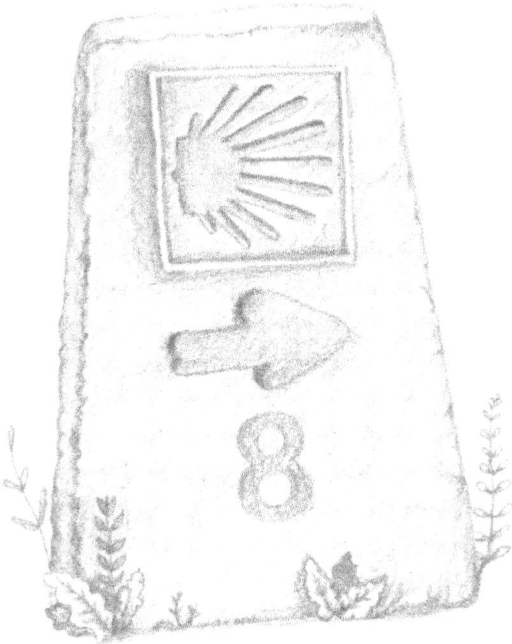

Dear Miyoung and Jamie

Even as I greet you, I need to think carefully to remember which one is which! Not because you are indistinguishable, or not unique, but because I hold you collectively as the 'Seoul Sisters'. Not biological siblings, but sisters in the similarity of your ways of being, in the spread of your smiles, the ease and warmth of your presence, your short shorts and pixie-like playfulness.

In my experience, the pilgrim scale typically tilts towards speaking, towards telling one's own story. A story often carried not just up the steep, sweaty climb from St Jean Pied de Port, and through the verdant hills and puffed up clouds of the Pyrenees, and along the path to Santiago, but a story whose company has been kept for a much longer time. Stories intricately threaded into the fibre of one's being, one's identity, yet stories that unintentionally lessen the space for new narratives to be written because the more of one's breath is held in the past, the less the air available to be breathed in the present.

You two of Seoul, so different to this. Something to do with East vs West? Or just a matter of nature or nurture? I don't presume to know, how could I? But I did see, feel, touch – your presence, wholehearted, full-bodied, yet with a feathery liveliness, and your appetite for living and knowing, as healthy as your appetite for food. Not the high intensity, high maintenance of Spanish David and his backpack full of questions about life and the universe, questions he held tightly with a 'must know'. Your questions, held with openness, and a curiosity that buzzed in the lightness of your being.

How astonished I was by your dinner table, covered corner to corner, a complete antithesis to the sterile smooth yellow surfaces of the albergue's kitchen. A large pan of sizzling pork, steaming rice, bright red tomatoes, a generous bowl of *kimchi*. So surprised you were to find here, in the village of Cacabelos, this staple of Korean cuisine, salted and fermented vegetables. Even more surprised, to learn that the shopkeeper from whom you bought the *kimchi*, had a South Korean girlfriend. She too, perhaps once a pilgrim? But more astonishing to me, than the volume of food destined for your slight frames, the watchtower-like bottle that cast its cool gaze from the corner of the table. How you laughed at my enquiry about the *vino tinto* that overlay my assumption that you didn't drink wine.

"The most important part of the meal" said Jamie, "more important than the *kimchi*!"

It was not just sights and smells that you brought to the kitchen, but being, and bounce, to the staid beige tiles and fluorescent light. The open door to the dull, grey, concrete of the back yard, wholly ineffectual in bringing any fresh air into the confines of the kitchen. Allowing instead an oozing heat released from the raindrops landing among the empty beer crates, and abandoned washing line. Beige, bland, but a quiet place, just a low hum from a distant TV. A place that held the possibility of my supermarket provisions being arranged into a meal of my choosing. A quiet place, until your arrival. A burst of sound, voices, and packets, as your energy enveloped the kitchen. You two, plus a third, the young South Korean called Song, who you adopted into your dinner preparation.

"Sorry", Jamie's word issued over the hissing, splattering pork.

An apology I usually only receive on it becoming known that I am vegetarian, but one given in your case, out of courtesy, not in response to knowledge.

"No problem", implied the smile from my mouth, closed behind a forkful of egg, mushroom, and onion.

We did not exchange many words that evening. A fuller conversation would come many days later. But it was most definitely a dance of energies. Mine which had been flat, with the heavy tread of a reluctant dance partner, disconnected from any inner rhythm, but which had become infected by your levity, laughter, and chatter, infused by the liveliness of the sizzling pork. How could I not but accept your unintentional offer, of joining you in the quickstep of your energies? Unintentional, because it was not by design or deliberateness, but rather about what my senses told me about your authentic, automatic selves – through your cooking, your connection to the kitchen, to each other, to me.

In addition to accepting the 'dance' you offered, my offer to you – two boiled eggs that I had made for the next day, but that had lost their appeal.

"Sorry", I said, "three of you, and only two eggs, but still one in the box, if you'd like to boil it".

Wide smiles of gratitude, and I thought, "It's only eggs!" Such a tiny offering, yet what you had made possible for me, a significant mood manoeuvre. A shifting in the flatness and disconnection, with which I had arrived at the albergue, a hangover from the greyness of the day, and the extra steps walked in the late afternoon drizzle to find a suitable bed. The emptiness of my 'conversation tank'.

Transformed by your energy and the connection, I stepped out of the albergue into the damp of evening. The drops now gentle companions, rather than the nuisance they were in my earlier downcast state. My feet no longer heavy, led me away from the main pilgrimed-street, into the residential parts of the village, past flowerpots and roses, and evening domesticity. I came to rest, in a village square café-bar, pen in my left hand, beer just to my right. Still enveloped in the warmth of your smiles, Jamie and Miyoung, and now also held in the gaze of a voluptuous beauty, looking down on me from the wall on which she had been so lovingly and largely painted. A figure that I might never have had the chance to admire, had I not encountered you two in the kitchen. An encounter, no doubt bestowed on me by the benevolence of the 'Camino Angels', in the spitty, spottiness of Cacabelos.

The same angels that sprinkled their dust on me, nearly a week later, in the early hours of a Palas de Rei morning. A village so heavily 'pilgrimed' that it was only on the fifth telephone call, that I had secured a bed, at an albergue on the outskirts of the village. An albergue to which I arrived late and spent the night, at a distance, not just from the life of the village, but also, from any conversation. My dinner for one, surrounded by human noises but not human connection. The cement-mixer crunching of tortilla crisps, the couldn't-care-less TV. No warmth of words at the end of a long day.

What a joy, as I approached the centre of Palas de Rei the following day, to hear:

"Sharon, Sharon!"

Waving arms, mile-wide smiles, clapping hands. A seven am breakfast, not at all my standard, but that day, a deliciously sweet treat. Not just once again, to be in the embrace of your energy, so welcome after the desolation of the night before, but between mouthfuls of the freshly baked chocolatey *napolitana,* to be fed parts of your stories. The biographical story of a teacher and an accountant, "36 and 38 in western age, and 34 and 37 in Korean age". The broader narratives – the stories of being a single thirty-something in Korean culture, stories of relationships with parents. Of fathers and mothers, much loved, but not always seen eye-to-eye with. Of parents and children with different exposure, differently travelled, with different interpretations of the world.

Continents apart in our upbringing, between your remote rural village, hours from Seoul, and my seaside town in the far south of Africa, yet togetherness in the stories of our being in these physical places, and being in relationship with our elders and their ways of seeing and being.

Another cup of coffee, and deeper explorations of what really mattered to us, on the Camino and on the other paths of our lives. Seriousness, but also fun. Floating on the sea of our laughter when we found a way of helping me tell you two apart – your names written large into my notebook, a side of the page held in each of your hands, a face next to the hand, and an arrow between your name and face. Click. Picture taken. Got it!

What a wrench to disentangle myself from the interweaving of our countries, callings, and conversation. To step out of the café-bar, and onto our separate schedules towards Santiago.

My future sightings of you would not be in person, but in pictures. On Facebook. Your joy-filled smiles and short shorts at Finisterre, the 'end of the earth' and the end of your Camino journey. Then pictures from Porto, and your transition from pilgrim to traveller, and finally pictures of you back in your motherland. Pictures of two very beautiful women in elegant dresses, and intricate jewellery, in sophisticated settings. The very same women who were so beautiful in their Camino simplicity, a beauty that had so wholeheartedly wrapped itself around me.

Thank-you, my Seoul Sisters, for bringing such soul, when I so needed it, on my path to Santiago.

Love and hugs

Sharon

Dear Muriel

Khaki sleeveless dress, pink scarf lightly draped across shoulders and neck, smooth brown legs, silver strappy sandals. A study in subtlety, and elegance, and containment. Somewhat out of step with the disorganised energy and discordant feel of Foncebadón.

On the shady side of the street, loud, dusty-looking pilgrims sat surrounding large empty beer glasses and overflowing ashtrays. On the sunny side, a slender wrist glided past a bowl of olives to the long-stemmed glass of white wine. Me, literally in the middle of the road, clean and contained, but certainly not elegant. My curiosity piqued by this picture of style and grace. Not likely a pilgrim, my assessment. But what would bring such a traveller to this remote, ragtag village? I was interested, but inward. Leave it be, you don't need to know. I continued my flat-footed, flat-mooded after-supper trudge around the village.

A day or two later, it's hard to be exact, because Camino days are longer than ordinary days, white shorts overtook me on the path. Shorts so 'other' than the hardy, multi-pocketed walking shorts that come in sensible shades of brown, grey, and dark green, or the quick drying black Decathlon sports shorts. These were white, loose flowing cheesecloth. Shorts that might more readily be associated with a 'Camino tourist', the rather disparaging label given by some hardened pilgrims, to walkers in running shoes, with daypacks. White cheesecloth, the last colour or type of shorts I'd ever choose to walk in. But, more surprising than the colour, the speed at which they were moving. No, the swift advance up the dusty hill, the full backpack, and deeply-browned calves, spoke of a seasoned pilgrim, or a person walking with a determination of purpose, striding away from something, or striving towards something. I didn't know which, and doubted that I would ever get to know, because the intensity of the pace was far beyond my steady gait. Like the 'Phantom of Foncebadón', another wondering stirred in me, another, that would not likely be answered.

A further interval of time and steps. A couple of hours out of Ponferrada, the white shorts appeared in my line of sight, and strangely, I was closing in on them. Was I walking faster? I didn't think so.

"Hello", I didn't think I'd ever catch you," I laughed.

"Why? I am not so fast." Mellifluous French tones, carried by playful butterfly wings.

"You are fast, believe me, but not so much now." I fell in step beside you, and so the entrée of your story was served. Muriel from Belgium. A walk started less than a week ago in Astorga, but a journey that had begun many months ago, two thousand kilometres back in France. The journey that might end for you in Santiago or in Finisterre, you were not yet sure.

We stepped at a good pace along the hard, flat tarmac in the undefined terrain between farmland and suburbia. Muted surrounds, good for conversation. An easy rhythm in the flow of our arms, legs, listening, and speaking. A measured sharing of information. A mouthful for you, a mouthful for me. Mindful chewing. Breath and spaciousness. No hurried gobbling of the starter or rush to large helpings of the main course of the story, a deeper story that you might or might not be carrying in your broad blue backpack, and that you might or might not choose to share with me.

"Hola, where are you from?"

The holler of a local man working in his garden, an interruption to the gentle ebb and flow of our speaking and silences. The Spanish-English sandwich not typical, especially not from someone of his years. A 'show and know'. He'd show, so that we would know about his knowledge of English. In his hands a long stem of lemon verbena that he placed under each of our noses, on his tongue, a long list of countries he'd visited. The lemon inhale, a sharp contrast to the rather bland surroundings. The speed and volume of his reciting, a loud contrast to the quite tones and spaciousness of our speaking. We laughed. It was hard not to, not to be captured by his exuberance, by his old-world-gentlemanliness. Would I have received the same enthusiasm, loquaciousness, and charm, had I passed his garden alone? Was there a difference in being two? A different level of engagement and chivalry offered to me because of walking alongside you, and your elegance-in-motion?

The lemon verbena tucked into the shoulder straps of our backpacks, we made our silent way into the next village, an unspoken contracting of turning down the volume after the noisy charm offensive of the Spanish gent. You were keen to stop to eat, and I not, so it was an easy separation of our steps. A thank-you for the gentle conversation and companionship, for the mouthfuls of stories shared. An *au revoir* without expectation of more.

Another passage of time and days of our separate steps along the path.

The Albergue El Paso in the tiny village of Vega de Valcarce. A rain-soaked evening, bookending a drippy day. The heavy grey, suddenly flecked with lightness as the sounds of your butterfly wing voice flapped gently into my ears, as you spoke with Maria, the kindly *hospitalera*. This time, not white shorts striding straight ahead, but denim ones, and a pirouette that greeted my greeting.

"Sharon here you are!"

Your lit-up face and clapping hands brought colour and energy to both the kitchen and me. Your need at the end of a long, wet day's walk was for something more nurturing than an albergue, so Maria told you where you could find a private room.

"Would you like to meet later for dinner?" you asked.

"No", I pointed at the giant marrow and enormous onion standing on the kitchen counter, products of Maria's labour, yanked out of the damp soil by her strong hands, an offering towards the dinner I was going to cook. "Would you like to join me?"

"Yes", you said, or at least I thought you did. You'd see me in a while, once clean and rested.

Onions, mushrooms, marrow, red pepper sizzled in the pan. The pasta cooked, places set at the end of the long table, fresh bread broken, ready. The juicy dessert peaches washed and cooling in the fridge. Something different about cooking for two. A joy in being able to offer to another, to give, to feed, something universal in this. Not being sure what you'd like to drink to accompany the meal, I decided to ask on your arrival, and then we could go the nearby shop together.

I sat and waited. The wait stretched, my stomach protested. Empty after the day's walking, tortured by the cooking smells hanging heavily in the humid kitchen. Seven o'clock became seven-thirty, crept towards eight. Bugger. Had something been lost in language? A disappointment rounded in over my shoulders. Did I wait longer? Did I eat? Neither, I went to the shop to buy beer for myself, to accompany what seemingly would now be *la cena sola*.

Back. Pasta scooped into the bowl, a healthy helping of vegetables heaped, a drizzle of olive oil, a generous coating of cheese. A delicious swallow of the cold golden *Mahou*. Eyes closed, I breathed deeply into the rich smells, the wait over, accepting my 'dinner-for-one'.

Eyes re-opened. A loose flowing khaki shirt, a fine textured pink scarf. In front of me, not just Muriel of the white shorts and lemon verbena shoulder strap, but the elegant 'phantom of Foncebadón'. Your scarf not actually pink, but silky cream with the finest strands of cerise to give an impression of pink. Your shirt now, the same colour as the sleeveless dress of the carefully contained woman who sipped white wine and ate olives, who added a touch of decorum to the ragtag high village. Khaki and pink, your evening colours to the white and denim of your days.

"I've just dished, I didn't know if you were still coming."

"You cooked for me?" Surprise, delight.

"Yes, I thought that's what we'd agreed." Your understanding, that I would cook and eat, that you would come after.

How did we get this so wrong I wondered? We laughed. Of course, you'd love to eat, and so we did, sharing the pasta and Maria's garden-fresh vegetables. Sharing in the stories of us. Your 2000 kilometres of walking from France. Your work in the media business in Belgium. Your being mother to four teenage daughters.

But the fuller tastes and flavours of the stories, and more particularly your story, would come in further sittings, slowly, in the venturing into the deeper recesses of your words and emotions. The story of your thousands of steps from France – steps that began in the dark of winter, the dark night of your soul. The sudden ending of 25 years of what you had thought to be a good marriage, to the man who was not just your beloved husband and best friend, but a wonderful father to your four daughters. A man who you'd thought you knew, but who'd declared the marriage to be over, that he had found someone else. Your incomprehension so strong, that all you could do was walk. To be in action, to be in your body, anywhere but in your head or heart. And so, your walking began, in the north of France, not with any hope of understanding, but with speed and fierceness, the hope of distraction.

Now, eight months later, you were walking again, continuing on the path, but a path that was slowly and quietly beginning to offer the possibility of a different way of walking and, to my observer, a different way of being.

Why or how could I have said this? You might ask. Did I make a study of you?

No, not a study, but simply my noticings over the time that we had been together. The furiousness of your initial pace, a pace that I could nowhere near match. Yourself sitting apart in the fading light of Foncebadón. Quiet, contained. The easing of your pace, *poco poco*, the emergence of your story, and its more heart-wrenching chapters. The journey into your emotions, the place furthest from you at the start of your 2000 kilometres. The closer you got to Santiago, the slower you walked, and the more fully you occupied the space of emotion, a place I sensed was too raw, too sore, for you to allow yourself into before. Now you were listening and feeling into this space, prying open a small window and allowing others to see the pain and confusion behind the elegance and containment.

The journey, as I heard and witnessed it, from the darkness and devastation of what you were walking from, into the possibility of a different future. A walk that began in heavy winter clothing and traversed into the height of the Spanish summer. From heavy jacket and woolly hat to white shorts and silk scarf.

I noticed how tired this process seemed to have made you, but that you stayed with it, honoured it with your full presence. Your day and a half stop at Mercadoiro, a testament to this. A private establishment along the path. A big garden and a gentle energy, and not much else. Nothing really to do there, other than to be. An important place in your processing, an important place on your journey to Santiago and beyond.

How my heart danced when I saw your outstretched arms and outstretched smile, felt the combination of your bursting energy and serenity, as you stood on the Praza do Obradoiro, under the majestic gaze of the cathedral of Santiago. How fitting to see you clothed, not just in your white shorts, but a light sleeveless white top, and white socks above your hiking boots. And more than that, Muriel, to notice your left hand holding your straw hat, and your right hand open, fingers widespread. One hand holding onto what mattered, the other, a reflection of having let go, on your long road to Santiago, that which you had held and been held by, a release that now created space and possibility, towards a different future.

Thank you, Muriel for the gentleness of your company, and for letting both me and you, walk into the fullness of your story.

May the path ahead continue to be lighter, whiter, and slower, than it was before.

Warm wishes

Sharon

Hola Angela

August, Spain's hottest month. Supposedly. Clearly, Galicia didn't get the memo. Bleak, grey, the biting wind as fierce and unfriendly as a False Bay South Easter. A coastal wind, Angela, that blows her thick, salty-sticky breath heavily against one's skin, against one's wellbeing. A wind not dissimilar to that which teased me up the grinding eight kilometres from Las Herrerias to O Cebreiro, a constant cold prickle on my face, a steady sweaty trickle from neck to navel in the steam of my windbreaker. A tease, that became a torment, as the imagined respite from the angry wind, once I reached the top of the mountain, did not come. Galicia, a province of her own mind. *Duvka*. A fitting Hebrew label to hang around her neck. "Just to annoy, just to be contrary".

The wind somehow colder, more menacing on the other side of O Cebreiro. Twelve long, crunching, kilometres to Fonfría, to your village, my overnight stop. Kilometres made longer, not only by the swirling schizophrenic wind, unable or unwilling to blow in just one direction, but also by the tar road running alongside the path. A road with kilometre markers to taunt tired pilgrims, markers that make progress feel even slower. Eventually, the five houses that constitute the village of Fonfría, and the Albergue A Reboleira, your albergue, Angela. A place of warmth and wholeheartedness, a feast for my senses, for the sixteen hours of my stay.

On previous paths, I had not lingered long in Fonfría, just a short pause to poke my head in at A Reboleira and greet you. Not because I knew you, Angela, but because I knew someone who knew you. Pamela from Cape Town. A Camino common denominator. A passionate pilgrim whose thousands of steps over ten Caminos, have woven together a world wide web of stories and song lines. A woman equal in heart and soul to you, Angela.

"Where is she? The friend of my friend?" The loud laugh in your voice.

Whereas before, I had sought you out to convey a Cape Town hug, this time, it was me who was sought, and squeezed tight against your friendly breast. Soft skin so warm and welcoming, after the cold, largely unconnected day. A holding, that held its ground and took its time, that grounded me. I didn't know that you even knew I was there. I hadn't announced my arrival, or declared my connection to your son as he checked me in. All I'd asked was whether the communal dinner had garlic, and the possibility of a meal without.

"I'll ask the chef." His single sentence.

Was the South African passport enough for him to join the dots, or more accurately, to join the hearts? Of you, me, and Pamela? A joining that led to an immersion – me into the deliciously generous embrace of your strong arms and soft breast? An embrace as generous and delicious as the dinner you would later serve me. A dinner indeed, *sin ajo*, without garlic.

A short chilly walk down the windy path, a brief reminder of the harshness of the day. A walk into what in Africa, we call a *rondavel*, a large circular dwelling, with a conical roof. Into the warmth and weave of a communal pilgrim dinner. At least thirty pilgrims seated on either side of the long wooden table. The air thick with end-of-day energy – a gratitude to have arrived, to be warm and clean, to be in community, among the battalions of red wine and water, stationed on the green and white checked tablecloth, about to be fed.

The *plato primero* delivered to the table. Giant bowls of Galician soup, and baskets of dark crusty bread. Me, in the wondering, my always wondering, *lleva ajo*? Did the soup carry garlic? The ever-present ingredient, so loved by most, so disliked by my senses and stomach. A large silver bowl appeared UFO-like over my right shoulder, beyond it, an even larger grin.

"Sharon, for you, *sin ajo*".

My very own bowl! Childlike delight at this unexpected gift. My insides warmed before even one swallow of the steaming spinach and potato soup reached my hollow stomach. A small swallow, and then a deep dive into the hot broth, each mouthful a softening of the hardship of the day.

The soup cleared, more wine sloshed into the squat tumblers, the arrival of the *platos segundos*. Vast platters of brown beef stew and gleaming white rice. For the vegetarians, single multi-coloured servings. Red, white, green, and yellow – peppers, rice, broccoli, and egg. Heavenly in its simplicity, generosity, and nutrition. An offering of such love and care, feeding body and soul.

How you do it Angela, I just don't know. Not only the generosity, and seeming joy with which you give, but also, the consistency of the giving. Each night, a different population of pilgrims for whom you provide not simply a bed and a meal, but a warm-hearted home. What love radiates from behind your well-worn apron and simple blue sleeveless T-shirt. From a way of being that says, "take me as I am". No dress up, no pretence, a complete comfort in your own skin. A way of being that equally says, "I take you as you are."

How noticeably different, at least to my observer, you are, from those seated at your long tables. People at different stages in their journey into finding ease, acceptance, and comfort in their own skins. Pilgrims seated around me with whom I have stepped, had salt-and-pepper sprinklings of interaction, or observed from a foot's length along the path.

The Englishwoman who sits opposite me, part of a pack of pilgrims at least fifteen years younger than herself. A woman, whose loud voice and louder laugh, have rung in my ears and grated on my nerves. A voice and laugh that to me, belie something deeper, quieter – a yearning to be liked, to be accepted. Accepted by others, because this is less difficult than being accepted by herself. A woman, Angela, who in the warmth of your food, and the warmth of your way, I see a little differently, through kinder eyes. A little less judgment, a little more compassion for what she's carrying in her backpack of life. I learn her name. Karen. Next to her, another Karen. Dutch Karen, whose cellphone's pumping music scratched roughly on my already prickly skin up the steep, windswept climb to O Cebreiro.

"Listen on bloody headphones", the mouthing of my irritation as I tramped past her.

Now, in the warm web of the *rondavel,* I listen to her words, to the story of her immense struggle up the hill, the saviour that was the 'thumper thumper', without which she would most certainly have surrendered in a desperate, tearful heap. I listen to the many other stories poured out with the never-ending bottles of red wine.

Had I become someone else at the close of the day? Had my own way shifted somewhat Angela, because of being held in the generosity of your love and care? In being part of the wondrous web you weave?

Postres. Santiago tart. Sweet, crumbly, coconutty. More conversation and connection.

The *rondavel* suddenly swallowed by the sound of samba. Your apron came off. Arms, legs, hips, and huge smile advanced towards the table. Nothing more was required in terms of an invitation. The dancing, such wonderfully different steps to the twenty-five thousand or so taken that day to get me to where I was. Samba steps with an icing sugar coating of laughter, lightness, and playfulness. I asked after your husband, remembering you being married to a Brazilian. Perhaps the source of the samba?

"He's gone. Left five years ago, it's better that way". Acceptance, no bitterness.

"He left you the samba", I say with a wry smile.

"Yes, and I love it, it will never go, even if he did." We float in your laughter.

Many sambas later, I ask if we could go to Africa.

"Si, si, claro" as you pointed me to the iPad behind the long bar counter.

Tap and type. The *rondavel* now captive to the booming base of Mandoza. Spain, UK, Holland, Germany, we moved to the distinctly South African sound.

A first for Fonfría? I can't be sure. But what I can be sure of Angela, my absolute joy of being in that moment, of being in your presence and in your place, a place that after a hard day, brought me back in step with this moving community of pilgrims, back in step with myself and my humanity.

How grateful I am Angela, for your holding, for the heart you shared with me on that day and have shared so abundantly with the great many that have come before me, and that you will no doubt share, with the great many still to come.

Muchas gracias por todos.

Un abrazo fuerte

Sharon

Dear Alvaro

Conflicted. The word that comes when I think of you. Still, these months later. Conflicted. In my thoughts, my feelings, my body. Held in one hand, a depth of compassion for what you have struggled with and overcome, the things that someone of your 17 years should not have had to. In the other hand, an equal depth of discomfort, disappointment, despair.

"Intelligent decisions are those made by the brain."

The first words I heard from your lips. Such vehemence. Somewhat out of sync with the lightness of the casual conversation of the communal dinner in Fonfría. Vehemence, more typically transmitted from the cynicism of many years lived, not by a teenager. The force of your tone, a trigger for my curiosity, the 'on' switch for my enquirer.

"What about the heart, and its role in decision-making?" My light asking.

"No, only the brain can make good decisions. The heart is weak. Emotions make bad decisions."

The muscles on your face strained tight across your cheeks. Your jaw set firm under its light dusting of man-boy whiskers. 220V of electricity pulsing from your sinewy arms.

Aha, no point in pursuing this one. The immovability of the made-up mind. Not even the narrowest crack to let the light in. I sipped on my beer, you roughly sloshed more dark wine into your glass. Your mother, seated between you and I, dabbing gently against your sharp edges. A kind, knowing smile in my direction, and a whisper in my ear:

"He has his reasons." I nodded, returned her smile. For all your full-frontal fierceness, perhaps a slight rocking on your axis. A softer, less declaratory sentence, "I have a story."

Dessert arrived at the supper table. Santiago tart.

"I don't eat it, it's too sweet." Back to the forceful 'intelligent brain' tone. Another gulp of wine, another softening. "I can tell it to you, I can tell you my story. Later."

An hour later, we sat, swallowed by the beanbags in the lounge of Angela's albergue. Unusual seating, at an unusual place, at an unusual hour. It was after 10 pm and the lights were still on. Not the 10 o'clock curfew of most albergues. You now less intense. A bottle of sparkling water that hissed and fizzled earlier, as its lid was loosened at the dinner table. The water now stiller, as you started to slowly and softly pour your story into my listening.

The story of a brain tumour at the age of 13. The years of drugs that didn't succeed in their seek and destroy mission, but nearly succeeded in killing you, not in their toxicity, but in their devastating impact on your self and soul. Your brain completely inaccessible behind an impenetrable fog. Your only access, access to your emotions, drug-addled emotions that pulled you down, and declared your life not worth living. Years of suffering and torment. Three suicide attempts.

And then a year ago, an alternative to the devilish drugs. An operation to cut the cancer from your brain. A new possibility, a new devil to the one you knew so well, or a saviour? Possibility without a shred of certainty.

A saviour it was, a successful cut that unshackled you from your suffering, breathed new life into your body, placed your now abled brain at the left, right, and centre of your reborn being.

I got it. The swing of the pendulum to its furthest point. The banishing of your emotions, securely bolted out of every decision of the past twelve months. Twelve months of total dominance of the brain and its intellect. And yet Alvaro, like English Karen, who beneath her bluster, carried a low decibel desire, you too I sensed carried a quieter, deeper yearning. Yours, not to be liked or accepted, yours a yearning to cry, to become reacquainted with the emotions you had so successfully jailed for the last year. Your plaintive question to me late in the beanbag conversation, in the slow shedding of your brittle shell, in the whispered revealing of your vulnerability:

"Sharon, you of nine Caminos, tell me, will I cry on this Camino? I haven't yet. Will I cry between here and Santiago?"

A question you so desperately wanted for my lips to form into a 'yes'. A 'yes' that I simply could not give. All that I could give – my listening and my thanks. Thanks that came not from my brain, but from the very bottom reaches of my heart. A thank-you for entrusting me with your story. A story to be tucked into the precious pages of my journal, tucked away with my own story of this Camino, and all the Caminos that had come before it.

Conflicted.

The word I started with, many words ago, and to which I now return. Because, at the opposite end of my admiration and compassion for you, a seething anger, or more accurately perhaps, an anger that seethed at the time, that squeezed the breath from my chest, and clenched my fingers into arthritic claws. Yes, fierce words, Alvaro. A fierce reaction to you – to your anger, your judgment, and your superiority, when I met you again, on the heavily pilgrimed path beyond Sàrria.

"Today is shit!"

Your bitter greeting, as I came upon you at the tiny café-bar about eight kilometres from Sàrria. A café-bar slightly obscured from the main path, one that I had chosen to stop at in the hope of it being less overwhelming in noise and numbers, than the ones I had passed that morning. Your wiry frame radiating righteous indignation, as your long fingers worked black masking tape onto your sandals, sandals that the 700 kilometres of your walking had all but destroyed. Hungry open mouths under the balls of your feet. You noticed my noticing.

"I'll throw them away, walk barefoot, my feet are like leather."

A simple fact or a boast, I'm not quite sure, but what was sure, at least to my listening, the acidity of your tone. What sat beneath your acid tone and calloused feet? The hundreds of kilometres you'd tread and toiled from Saint Jean Pied de Port in the French Pyrenees. So much work done, such fierce commitment to the cause. A 'true' pilgrim, like others who'd travelled the long way. And now, today, the path filled with 'pretenders', not pilgrims. Not words from your lips, Alvaro, but meaning expressed by every ounce of your being, in the buzzing swarm of the Sàrria pilgrims.

"Yes", I said, not unsympathetic, having struggled myself with this, on previous Caminos. The volume of pilgrim traffic on this part of the *Camino Francés,* the last 100 kilometres between Sàrria and Santiago de Compostela. A distance walked that would entitle the issuing of a *compostela,* a certificate, from the pilgrim office in Santiago.

"This is a difficult day for the Saint Jean starters", I continued. "But these new people on the path, they also have a story."

"No. No they don't!" Your not-quite-man-yet voice, loud, adamant.

My jaw tightened, my breath quickened, a cold crept up my arms. My head, filled with the many people I've walked alongside, albeit briefly, on this part of the path. With the stories spoken and unspoken – heart wrenching tales of loss and grieving, of hope and aspiration. Stories securely, lovingly, painfully, hopefully, carried in day packs, over these 100 kilometres. Kilometres that are in truth, just a fraction of a far longer journey.

Beneath my anger, a deep woundedness, not so much for your implicit declaration of their unworthiness to be called 'pilgrim', but for your cruel branding of them as 'people-without-stories'.

"How can you say that? That they do not have a story?" I pressed my finger into your bare, bony shoulder, emphasising my point.

"That's arrogant!" Like you in your drug-induced fog, I now was nowhere near my brain, but completely catapulted into my emotions, into my anger, a place in which I am rarely immersed.

"Everyone has a story. You have a story!" A heart wrenching story, you shared, in a late-night conversation just two nights ago. "You cannot say that others do not have a story. That is a bad thing to say." My judgment now in full swing, in full voice, rising up to meet yours.

Game on, your body was rigid, but your language was limbering up. You then told me about the man you'd met that morning, in new clothes, freshly bought from Decathlon. A man who, in reply to your question of why he was walking, said "for sport and the *compostela*".

Evidence. An air punch I don't see but feel. Your tone victorious. A few breaths for me in the time of your telling, a slight dialling down of my anger.

"Yes, it may well be so, that this man walks the Camino for these reasons. Maybe that is where he finds himself now in his life."

But your mind was made up. An unnecessarily forceful hoist of your backpack onto your shoulders, and your bare feet stomped away from the café-bar.

I was left to my coffee and *napolitana*. The one bitter, the other sickly sweet. A short while later, I too hoisted my backpack onto my slumping shoulders. The anger gone, given way to a crushing disappointment and a heavy heart.

Why did I have to stop at that particular café-bar? Why did I have to have that interaction? As you well know, Alvaro, coffee breaks feed not just your body but your soul, and so with a bad one, disappointment. And with this particular one, not just disappointment, but a vast well of sadness.

My work then, to let go of the judgement I felt towards you, for the judgement you had fired off in piercing semi-automatic rounds. To walk in the very same question that I had asked you at the start of our discussion, before it became a debate, and descended into a duel.

"How much of your energy, do you want to give over to this mood? Energy that could be better directed into your walking?"

A question of the head, rather than the heart, or in your words, Alvaro, "of the brain rather than the emotions".

I made my sad, heavy way back onto the path, but in the spaciousness and quiet, my steps were no longer those of the boots-and-backpack being of a pilgrim, but the strong strides of woman in a black gown. A black courtroom gown of a criminal prosecutor, the prosecutor of a previous life, a prosecutor known for her cutting cross-examination and compelling closing arguments.

What came, incisive, carefully crafted questions that would have cast doubt on the credibility of your case, Alvaro. The critical unasked question that sat indigestion-like in my chest, that I addressed in a measured, firm voice, not to you, but to the small-eared flowers in the large empty field running alongside me:

"So, because this 'Decathlon man' walks for the reason he does, and you walk for the reason you do, does this make you a better person than him? Or only a better pilgrim?"

And, another aspect my prosecutor could have explored had her arrival been better timed:

"Even if the large groups of schoolchildren, church groups, families and weekend walkers are doing this 100-kilometre road from Sàrria to Santiago, for reasons and in ways less serious or committed than you, is this not, after all, their country? Are we not their guests?"

It was only many kilometres later, Alvaro, with my headphones on, that court went into recess, that my mood began its manoeuvre. The words of the singer James filled my ears, "Pleased to meet you. Where're you from and what's your name?"

I took this as a sign, that we were supposed to meet, when we met. Not just in the ease and blessing that was the night at Angela's albergue in Fonfría, but also in the intensity and anger of this day. That the 'Camino Angels' sent you. A fierce, defiant teacher, but a teacher, nonetheless? And in this knowing, I could step, somewhat lighter with less tightness in my chest, knees, and knuckles, along the afternoon path to Portomarín.

I would see you just once more, a few morning's later in Arzúa, about 40 kilometres from Santiago. A sighting of you and your mother, from the main street into the far corner of a café-bar. You hadn't seen me, so a decision had to be made of whether I would come in and greet you. A strong wave of antipathy washed over me, an emotional hangover I was still carrying. Should I, shouldn't I? I did, perhaps not with oozing enthusiasm or an acknowledgment of having been 'pleased to meet you'. But with a simple "hello" and a "*Buen Camino*" for your remaining kilometres to Santiago and the completion of this part of your journey.

I am not sure, Alvaro, if your deep yearning was met, your yearning to cry before reaching Santiago, to be reconnected with the emotion you had so completely banished for the preceding year. My suspicion is that you did not cry, most likely, because your head wanted it too desperately. But maybe, in some wholly unexpected place, and a wholly unexpected time, a memory or moment of the Camino might have been triggered, and in that moment, tears might have come, entirely on their own terms, tears from the heart, and not tears from the head. And maybe, that moment is still to come.

For your onward journey, I wish you well, in head and heart.

Sharon

Dearest Dorothy, Eleanor, Cate, and Svetlana

It is interesting that I should have felt, and have been spoken to by your professions, before any words about your worlds of work were spoken, before any descriptions given. All four of you in service of others, albeit in somewhat different ways. A women's centre for the healing arts in Germany, an NGO in northern Uganda that employs and empowers victims of trauma, capacity building of social workers in Macedonia, years of service to humanity across many continents through a kinder, saner, more humane US government.

How much I needed you four, your holding, and healing, the day I first met you on the path between Sàrria and Portomarín. How much I needed your gentle balm to calm my angry rash-red skin, to settle my acid-churned stomach.

You were not immediately four, but to begin with, two. Two women I encountered on a swarming stretch about 15 kilometres beyond Sàrria. One woman tall, one shorter.

"How's your walk going?" No "Hola" or "Hablas Ingles?" before I interjected my question into the flow of your steps and speaking.

"Fine thank-you", the polite, light reply. My sensing, that you expected me to move on, but I didn't, instead shortened my stride, slowed my pace to fall in step alongside you. Quiet moments passed, more steps taken.

"I wondered if you might be feeling some discomfort? Carrying a bit of a niggle in your body?"

"Actually, yes, what makes you ask?" The taller of two replied, the one with walking poles and a cheerful floral shirt.

"A few things", my reply. I explained my noticing. The slightly uneven gait, the somewhat tentative foot placements, a leaning on the walking poles.

"Is it that noticeable, the discomfort, my achy knees?"

"Probably not to most", I smiled. Most pilgrims, in my experience, are more attuned to their own bodies, focused on their own progress along the path.

A short story, I shared.

Three Caminos ago, a 450-kilometre journey. For 400 kilometres, my body, a well-oiled walking machine. Smooth, gliding, efficiency. Then 50 kilometres of painful tendinitis that halved my pace and quartered my spirit. Why now? Why, when I'd been walking so well, with such fluidity and ease? And within that final 50 kilometres, an excruciating two kilometres down the mountainside from Monte do Gozo to the outskirts of Santiago. A stretch so joyful to most, Santiago in sight, but so agonising for me. A cruel descent that reduced me to penguin steps. But way beyond the stabbing pain between my right shin and ankle, the searing pain of invisibility. My pain, totally unseen and unacknowledged by the throng of pilgrims making their single-sighted way to the cathedral of Santiago.

Eventually, as the mountain began to moderate her severe slope, the offer of Voltaren from a gentle Swedish pilgrim. A woman I'd been in quiet community with, but never actually spoken to. As the Voltaren breathed its hot breath on my screaming shin, I cried, not for the agony, but for her kindness, for her seeing, for her acknowledgement.

This is maybe why I noticed, noticed the signs of discomfort, discomfort that, in the physical demands of this path, so easily becomes pain.

"Thank-you for your noticing, and for your asking." Soft brown eyes, cat-like in their narrowing, rested upon me.

"Thank-you for your listening," my reply.

A smile, a nod and a *Buen Camino* as I increased my stride. Silence now behind me, and then the resumption of your conversation. My step and spirit a little lighter, an easing in the chafing against my sensitive skin, the chafing of the interaction with angry Alvero.

The path, noisy and crowded, under the densely clouded sky. Backpacks and bodies, like a bloated just-fed puff adder, snaked their way between the 'higgeldy-piggeldy' stone walls that held between their corners, lazy brown cows, and bright yellow daffodils. Time to be immersed in the sounds of my own choosing. The throaty strains of John Martyn, and thoughts of my dear friend Jane, the remembering of my 50th birthday, and this very piece she played in our celebration circle. John Martyn's growl gave way to the more animated tone of James. "Pleased to meet you, where're you from and what's your name?" I was probably singing out loud, I didn't care, I was grateful for a different expressing, happy and wholesome, a strong contrast to my breakfast stop outburst, so acrimonious, so uncharacteristic.

Onward and downward, I stepped into a buzzing beehive of pilgrims just beyond Mercadoiro. Pilgrims drawn to hundreds of brightly painted conch shells, lining the outside walls of the wayside shop. I, in turn, was drawn to two women pausing in the middle of the path, surveying the shells from a distance. One taller, a red and blue checked shirt, the other, shorter, in a pale blue T-shirt. Wide-brimmed beige hats, and multi-pocketed lightweight walking pants. Women who struck me, in their silent stillness, as women of substance, maturity, and groundedness. Not because of the clothes they wore, or my reckoning of their sixty-something years, but in their energy and presence. Energy and presence that talked to solidity and self-knowledge. Women that my conversationalist yearned to meet, but in a place of breath and breathing space, not there in the buzzing beehive. So, as the women stepped on, I paused, surrendered to a six-striped rainbow conch shell, and its call to accompany me to Santiago.

A couple of kilometres later, at a sharp corner in the road, and tucked tightly beside it, a bench, under small rectangle of wooden roof. Almost past it, when my eye was caught. A scene so reminiscent, so poignant, my breath stopped. I came to an abrupt halt. The bare foot of an outstretched leg rested lightly on a lap, cradled by tender fingers that attended to a blister or a burning. But this wasn't Pam and Elke in the verdant green garden at the Refugio Guacelmo in Rabanal del Camino. It was the two blue-shirted women of my earlier conversationalist's curiosity.

"Hello", as I took a step closer. "I know this is going to sound really strange, and you can say no." I paused. No movement, stillness, waiting.

"Would you mind if I took a picture?" Slightly uncertain smiles, cautious agreement.

The moment captured, with a constricting throat and breaking voice, I began my explanation. I introduced the two pilgrims in front of me to two pilgrims they did not know, two Canadian pilgrims I carry so warmly and deeply within my heart, and have carried since 2013, both on and off the path. And so it was, Dorothy and Eleanor, that you met Pam and Elke, learned their names, even before you learned mine, or I learned yours.

After this unconventional beginning, the strands of our conversation started to braid themselves together. Not in any biographical order, but simply starting in that moment and dancing lightly here and there. I felt moved to share with you, Dorothy and Eleanor, the joy and meaningfulness of my brief interaction with two women a short while before. Women I was pleased to meet, but whom, unlike James, I had not asked: "Where're you from and what's your name?" Women whom I had simply seen, and been seen by, and this was indeed, enough.

"Was one tall with long brown hair, walking with two poles, and the other shorter?" inquired Dorothy.

My "yes" met with a beam and twinkling eyes.

"That's Cate and Svetlana, the other two of our walking party. Actually, we're waiting here for them, we got a bit ahead of them."

Was I surprised? No, a separation of a couple of kilometres, but very similar ways of being and energies, of presence, and groundedness, of listening, and spaciousness. Not surprised, but delighted, something so special for me in having met all four corner pieces of your Camino puzzle.

A specialness acknowledged by the universe. An impromptu blessing. The heavens opened, just after Cate and Svetlana's arrival at the bench. No option other than to huddle under the tiny patch of roof, us five, and maybe ten other pilgrims, generating warmth and wonder in the leaking greyness of the Galician afternoon. And what warmth was placed in the palm of my cold hand, a thimble-size conch shell on a fine leather strap.

"For you Sharon, for your noticing, for your care." Cate's hands lovingly cupped mine.

The rain no longer stamping, but tiptoeing, we five made our way carefully, companionably along the path, adding more pieces to our now collective puzzle.

Across the misty bridge and up the ancient stone steps. The parting of our ways at the entry into Portomarín. You four to your private lodgings, and me, to where, I didn't know. Given the volume of pilgrim traffic, what I did know, was that finding a bed in an albergue, would be difficult. A task, that at the end of an 'ordinary' day's walking can be draining, and how much more could it be, at the end of a day of such emotional intensity? Yet, despite the many *completos* that greeted me in my search for a bed in the bursting village, my search was through eyes of optimism and knowing. Knowing that I would eventually find something, a search buoyed by the gift of our connection and kindredness.

Buoyancy that not only found me a room, but also found me a quiet table at a hillside café-bar in the company of the evening sun. A sun that warmly caressed my cheeks, as I slowly sipped my beer and processed my day through penning a piece called 'Judgement Day at the Gates of Sàrria'. A piece I shared with you, Dorothy, the recipient of the email, and the appointed reader to your group, one lunchtime, a day or two later.

The next morning, a deliciously, decadent departure from Portomarín. The lateness, not occasioned by having a 10 am private room check-out time, as opposed to the 8 am albergue whip-cracking. Nor made possible because of the peace of mind of a bed already booked for the coming evening. But mostly, because Eleanor, Svetlana, Cate, and Dorothy, I dearly hoped to have a little more time with you four, you, who had now become known to me as 'the Famous Four'. Because, by my reckoning, having stayed privately and walking the way between Sàrria and

Santiago in half stages, you'd be slow out of Portomarín's starting blocks.

So, I did indeed linger long at the same hillside café-bar, enjoying the clarity of the morning sun across the broad blue expanse of the dam below, now unveiled from the previous day's mist. Savouring every mouthful of the aromatic coffee, the thick toasted *pan* with *marmelade*, the smooth harmonies of Fleetwood Mac coming from the TV suspended high in a far corner. An extremely unusual Spanish TV, my kind of TV, one set on a music channel.

"*Un television bueno,*" I remarked to the café-bar owner with a smile.

"*Sola musica, todos los demas canales mal.*" Music only, all other channels bad, she agreed.

Was it 11 o'clock by the time I left? An ungodly, 'unpilgrimed' hour to be setting foot onto the path. Pack on my back, sticks in my hands, a last look right up the hill towards the village square before a left turn onto the path. Four figures advancing down the road, moving towards me.

"It's Sharon, there you are!" Cate's arms waving enthusiastically.

Me, like my six-year-old self, standing in front of the huge silver Pick 'n Mix bowls in Garlick's department store in Claremont. Standing in anticipation of the deliciousness to come. A rare treat for my older sister and I, to dip into the big bowls with their colourful, shiny individually wrapped jewels. Chocolate-coated toffees, peppermint crisp, chocolate-covered marshmallows, Turkish delight, coconut ice. Bowls of possibility, bowls of wonder. And, in that moment in Portomarín, a similar excitement at the possibility of more delicious unwrapping.

Off we stepped. Sharing our stories, uncovering points of connection across continents and callings, meaning and purpose. Oh, the wonderful weaving of our words, along this Spanish way.

Then it was time to bid you all farewell, not because our brown packets of treats were all gone, but because you were drawn to a deviation, to visit a Romanesque church off the path, and then on to the end of your stage at Ventas de Naron, while for me, it was onward to Palas de Rei.

Uncertainty of whether any more treats would be shared or exchanged. But absolute certainty in my gratitude for the sweetness given and received, in the speaking and the listening, the seeing and being seen. And, all this offered and held, not in the outstretched hands and hearts of 'St Jean pilgrims', but in the abundance of three '100-kilometre pilgrims' and one '170-kilometre' one. Pilgrims so richly storied, and every bit as worthy, as any other pilgrim, to be on this path; to be called 'pilgrim'.

There would be just one more brief unwrapping, a few treasured moments with Cate, on the closing night of my 2019 Camino. But an unwrapping that has continued with its own ease and rhythm in the interconnectedness of our lives off the path. Some pictures and stories shared of my recent trip to Kampala, capital of the country of Dorothy's NGO, a sharing of my blogs and your websites. Yours, the only pilgrim connection of this 2019 Camino that has endured.

Cate, Eleanor, Dorothy, and Svetlana, I thank you for being there on a day I needed you so, a day that for me held such ugliness, complexity, and contradiction, a day that in your care and containment became one of such colour and beauty, a shifting and settling, a kaleidoscope of hearts, minds, and meaning.

Until we connect again

Sharon xxxx

H*ola chicos*

I cannot greet you individually by name, because I cannot remember your names. Not because I did not regard them as important enough to remember, but because our connection was not based on spoken words or the unwrapping of stories, as it was with 'the Famous Four'. My connection with you, 'the Spanish Four', was a connection of energies, a communication though eyes, hands, and hearts, a companionship lived, rather than 'languaged' in our steps along the pilgrim path.

I'm not sure where along the way it was, that the edges of our energies first lapped gently against each other's, somewhere beyond Astorga. But I do know that it was in the makeshift kitchen-cum-dining area at the Albergue Compostela, in the streamside village of Molinaseca, that a much closer overlapping occurred.

Molinaseca, a village of great charm and beauty, a place of polarity in my previous experiences. My first visit, a place of significance – sunset, supper, and stories, a small circle that cemented deep and enduring connections. My next visit, a few years later, the village objectively beautiful, but subjectively barren for me, no bed found, no bonds made. Instead, a heavy tarmac trudge to Ponferrada, and the madness and alienation of the 175-bed Albergue San Nicolas.

How wonderful it was this time, *chicos*, to find this lovely albergue. Especially so, after the mental and physical drain of the day's stage. Wicked bone-rattling descents from the Cruz de Ferro, dropping through the high village of El Acebo, and down further still, until the grateful appearance between the tall trees, the village of Molinaseca. Descents that severely punished bad knees and troubled hips, and whose steepness, loose rocks, and long smooth stony tongues, demanded fierce care and concentration. How reliant I was on my 'Black Diamond' walking poles, to support my safe passage. How extraordinarily demanding this path must have been for one of your four, *chicos*, the one who has just one arm.

About two kilometres before I was to reach Molinaseca, as the rocks and stones had begun to give way to a brown, sandy, but still sloping path, an unfathomable racket exploded from behind me. Booming voices and an almighty rattling of items bumping roughly against each other. The rattling and clattering growing louder, coming closer. Instinctively, I jumped off the path, for self-preservation, to avoid the still unknown avalanche. A jumble of arms, legs, and language, as two pilgrims came hurtling past. Not lithe, lean, light-footed trail runners with aerodynamic, body-hugging packs, but two burly bodies, bulging biceps and chaotic backpacks. A running shoe dislodged from a side pocket, landing grenade-like off the path just ahead of me.

Skidding, shouting, a mushroom cloud of dust, as the bigger of the two took a tumble, taken by surprise by a sharp rocky curve. He couldn't brake fast enough, his momentum too great. He was up quickly, a heavyweight boxer subjected to a left hook, but just a momentary kissing of the canvas. Unconcerned about the dust or any damage, oblivious to the projectile shoe, he was good to go.

"Oi, your shoe!" I pointed. Quickly retrieved, and stuffed hurried, insecurely, into the empty side pocket.

Peace restored. I returned to the path and continued into the village. Over the ancient stone bridge, past a few goose-pimpled swimmers, and then onward, to my discovery of the albergue, new in the three years of my absence. A peaceful place with the heavenly option – a bed or a bunk. A bed in a quiet dorm room. Heavenly indeed, but cruelly short-lived. Familiar voices, booming under the wide expanse of sky, positively cacophonous under the eaves in the containment of the dorm. Into my line of sight, a bald bowling-ball head, broad tattooed shoulders, a heavy silver chain, a grazed and slightly bloodied knee. No mistaking the testosterone-charged tumbler making his way towards a bed in the partition adjoining mine.

"OH FUCK!" my shouting thought, but instead "you got injured, you okay?" my spoken words as I pointed at his knee.

His chest puffed out impossibly further, "fine, fine, no problem."

"Macho man", my ironic response.

"Spanish man", his counter. Immediate, unequivocal, a simple statement of fact.

Spanish man and his mate proceeded to overpower the once quiet dorm. Everything about them, high decibel, disregarding. The door to the men's bathroom left open during their showers. Loud voices, even louder peeing. Mercifully, a respite as they went out for a late lunch, leaving me in contemplation of whether they were indeed, 'Spanish men'. In prayer, "Please God, let their lunch be long."

My head wilted onto my postage stamp traveling pillow. A full-bodied exhale, the sweet thought of a short siesta. Whoosh, the door swung open. Like Arnold Schwarzenegger, they were back, not just one terminator, but two. Rolled-over shorts, sleeveless low-cut vests. Men approaching fifty, with something to prove?

A few words exchanged between them and then an ear-numbing cell phone call, never mind me and the two German women trying for a much-needed nap.

"Por favour" I eventually pleaded, *"habla en vox baja"*. A broad goofy grin, a wave of his hand, the lowering of his volume, for which I was enormously grateful. Grateful that was, until his free hand seized a pair of nail clippers, and he set upon every nail on his fingers and toes. Each sharp clip, crystal clear above his dialled-down voice.

Spanish men, these two? Maybe, by their definition.

A very different definition from the one you four men offered to me, an entirely different way of being. Them, heavily jewelled, heavily tattooed, like electric guitar-wielding, aging rockers who dominate the centre stage in beams of fierce electric light and ego. Theirs, a 'Guns 'n Roses' way of being, to your 'Crosby, Stills, Nash, and Young'. Them, bold and brash, and self-involved. You, *chicos,* attuned, sensitive, respectful, in harmony with each other, and those around you. Qualities I experienced as you four sat down to eat a late dinner in the albergue's kitchen, as I sat down with my *te negro, chocolate con almendras,* and my notebook, in the damp, spotty fading of the day.

"Would you mind if we take this table, to use for our dinner, and you sit at the next table?" All this asked with arms and hands, and not words.

"Yes, of course" I smiled and slid myself and my things, one table to the left, along the row of three square tables under the large window. The end table lifted, placed soundlessly in the middle of the small room. Four squat metal stools posted to their new positions. No scraping, no bumping, no heavy-handedness. I pointed to the table to my left, empty, slightly obscured by a long hanging grey curtain. Then, more hand signals, to accompany my basic Spanish:

"Take my table too, you are four, and I am one. It is tight for four at one table. I can move along."

More smiles and hand gestures, as you insisted you were just fine around your single square.

A gentle hum of conversation, as you made your way through bread, *gamon,* and tomatoes, and on to your fruit, cut into neat squares, and covered with yoghurt. A swallow of my tea, I breathed into the ease and energy of our small kitchen island, into the welcome of my flowing black ink. As if on cue, a human loudhailer from the street below. The 'testosterone tumbler' beckoned to his fellow Spanish man to come down, so they could go out for dinner.

My eye caught the pair of black *broeks* I had pegged to the outside of the kitchen curtain, underwear I was optimistically trying to dry, under the uncooperative sky. A confession I had to then make to you four, that I had snuck my socks and T-shirt into the tumble dryer, a subversive sneaking amongst your full load of laundry.

"No problem", your smiles confirmed.

As quietly as you laid out your supper things, you then cleared them away and cleaned up. Collective action, an easy allocation of roles. Not a proper sink, but a handbasin for washing up. The kitchen, obviously a bathroom, in its pre-albergue life. A pokey basin that I had found awkward when washing the dishes from my simple supper of baked potato, cheese, and tomato. The basin at which, one of your foursome, was washing dishes. No noise, no fuss, no awkwardness that I could detect. The one of your four, who had just one arm.

The second time that day I was left marvelling, not just at his ability and agility, but at his being. Such a different 'Spanish man', actually, all four of you, so different, in my short observation, from what was declared to me earlier as being the "Spanish man". The respect that I felt pulsing ever so gently between the four of you, your spoken and quiet enjoyment of each other's company. Your care-filled regard for those around you. Walking the way, not dicing it. How different indeed, were your forty-something selves from the midlife menaces.

I bade you *buenos noches* and B*uen Camino* as I left the kitchen and made my way into the darkened dormitory. The two German women sound asleep. 'All quiet on the Western Front', but I still decided on evasive action, to decamp to a bed furthest from the so-called 'Spanish men'. A modicum of relief in the action taken, but I lay awake in the Chinese-water-torture-anticipation of their return.

A familiar whoosh as the door swung widely open, throwing light into the room. Slip-slopped feet slapped heavily across the wooden floor. More waterfall weeing splashed loudly from the open bathroom. At least my torture-tension had been broken.

Then at last, silence. How long until the snoring would start?

Start it did, but surprisingly, not from the bald bowling-ball, but from his less solidly built companion, a man lighter on his feet, lighter on the path, no tumbles taken. Albeit no snoring from the bowling-ball, I was not off the hook from him, noise-wise. From his corner, a Morse code of text messages, completely unheard by him in his heavy slumber, but each bleep, a stinging paintball-bullet against my frazzled form. I picked my way like a cat burglar, through the dark towards his bed, not to pocket a prized diamond necklace, but to nuke the bleeping offender.

Located, silenced with a firm finger. Relief.

The next morning, two gifts that greeted my waking. No sign of the two Spanish men, and my socks, atop my T-shirt waiting patiently for me on the kitchen table. Not just randomly plonked, instead, the T-shirt neatly folded, and the socks precisely placed one on top of the other. No doubt, carefully placed by you, the other Spanish men.

A couple of hours later, I would see you four in front of Ponferrada's magnificent *castilo*. I saw you from across the road, where I was having breakfast in a delightful coffee shop. My smile and wave were met by your four wide smiles and many waving hands. Smiles that somehow extended further as I took my phone out of my pocket, motioning my wish to take your picture through the large front window.

Some days later, on the path to Portomarìn, our energies would once again find each other's edges. I was walking among the words and ways of the 'Famous Four' in the grey dripping afternoon, when we paused to consider an *opcion* – two possible routes to be taken. In front of us, already in contemplation, two red ponchos, and two figures clad in black rain jackets and pants.

"What lovely men those are" as I pointed you four to this four. "I don't know their names or anything about them, but I do know how lovely they are."

And in the softness of that afternoon, it seemed a good time to ask your names, to tell you mine, and to take a picture, closer than the one taken through the Ponferrada coffee shop window.

"No," one of you said, "not a picture, a selfie."

With one picture, and one selfie taken, and an exchange of names, we were all on our way. Me with the 'Famous Four' along one *opcion*, and you four along another.

I would see you all just one more time. That same evening in Portomarín. Once again, you would sit close, and companionably, at a table alongside me. This time, you were eating pizza, while I sipped my quiet beer, letting my thoughts wander and slowly begin to organise themselves into sequence, between the lines of a clean, blank page.

The Camino holds many forms of communication and connection. How much I appreciated the subtlety, stillness, and smiles, of our largely unspoken connection. A connection felt, smooth to the touch, easy on the eye and ear. And how deeply grateful I was, for the beautiful example of a more benign way of being of 'the Spanish man'. A being so different from the one that had bombarded me and my senses in and around Molinaseca.

Saludos

Sharon

B*uenas dias* Luz

I know this isn't your name, but it's a name that feels right for you, for what you offered me. Light. Light, in the sense of lightness, of your gentle self, and the lightness of the beautiful *pasteleria* A Lua. 'A Lua', a Galician name meaning 'moon'. Your light, Luz, and 'The Moon', a soothing balm to my battle-bruised being, after my sixteen hours, besieged at the Albergue Ultreia, in the small village of Arzúa, forty kilometres from Santiago de Compostela.

Expectation is said to be 'disappointment waiting to happen'. Technically, not expectation in this case, but gratefulness and anticipation, that made the reality of my stay in Arzúa so heavy to bear. Deeply thankful to have secured a bed at the Albergue Ultreia, an albergue already *completo,* two days ahead of my call, but which, after the kind intervention of Cape Town pilgrim Pamela, I now had a bed. An intervention that literally brought tears of gratitude to my eyes, and an anticipated joy of staying once again, at this warm and wonderful albergue.

How welcome was my arrival at Ultreia, after a long 30 kilometres' stage, to be embraced by the quiet of the dark marble showers, the smooth blonde floors, ample armchairs, and mini chocolate wafers. An embrace that became such a delicious immersion, that I failed to attach any significance to the vast number of empty bunks, despite the lateness of the hour, an hour by which most albergue bunks would be awash with pilgrim possessions, or single stripes of snoozing sleeping bags. Little did I know, that a powerful *armada* of Spanish pilgrims was surging forward and would imminently occupy this peaceful place, and that my tears of gratitude would edge dangerously close to tears of frustration, as I became the collateral damage in the conquering.

What a relief it was, this morning, after my night with the *armada*, to find the clean white lines of the *pasteleria* A Lua, the large white display-shelves packed with their freshly baked breads and pastries, and the endless white countertop that extended the length of the cake shop. To feel a gentleness and care washing over me as I released my backpack from my slumping shoulders, and set it down against a straight table leg. To answer the whispered invitation of the crisp, white, pear-shaped chair, to sit down and be still, and to take as much time as I needed to recover my equilibrium.

A Lua was not an immediate find that difficult morning, but the third or fourth place I'd looked into as a potential stop, not just for the nourishment of coffee, but to nurse my wounded soul. The first four café-bars, directly on the path, and unappealing for various reasons. The first, on the main street, an overflow of *desayuno* detritus – empty plates with scoured out single-serving butter and jam containers, cups, and coffee-slopped saucers, surrounded by molehills of toast crumbs, and random coconut cookie wrappers. The second café-bar, clean and calm, but serving breakfast to the angry, young Alvero, whose hangover I was still processing. The third, too empty, and the fourth, too dark, cold, and cavernous.

A few steps up a narrow side street, away from the main path, away from the flood of pilgrims, the *pasteleria* A Lua presented itself. No television, just a steady stream of local patrons who made their purchases in friendly, even tones. No raised voices, nothing commanded or commandeered. And Luz, obvious to feel from my first moments in this sweet sanctuary, the warmth and welcome of your way. Despite your busy multi-tasking, eyes that saw me, and a soft smile that massaged my tight temples. Could you feel the fragility of my state as I approached you to order my coffee, your hands buried in the small sink, working your way over cups and dishes? Or do you send this concern and care to all your customers? Perhaps the latter.

I said I'd wait at the counter, and you could just pass me my *café solo* and accompanying cup of hot water, to save you a trip to my table. No, you insisted, with a tilt of your head, and a softening of your eyes, I should sit, and you would bring it. I duly deposited myself into the fat-bottomed chair, pulled my Iceland packet with my notebook and pen from the front of my backpack, and set it gently on the smooth square table.

I sat back and smelled deeply into the dark coffee you placed next to my notebook, and sniffed the sugary sweetness of the two freshly baked miniature 'pig's ears', you set down on a tiny saucer next to the espresso cup. Acts of service, acts of kindness. I held back on the pig's ears, to have them maybe later with my second cup.

How different this first interaction with you, Luz, from what had been my first contact with the *armada's* 'commander-in-chief', whom I had encountered, around 19h00, at the washing-line in the courtyard of the Albergue Ultreia.

"Bless you", my lightly issued offering after his cannonball sneeze. "You'll blow us to the next village along the way".

One of his subordinates, whom I assumed to be his daughter, translated, and so an inevitable time lag, a blank space between transmission and reception. The message received, his blankness replaced by the elongation of his mouth, as if pulled longer and downward by a small weight at each end. An absolute focus on his washing, the intentionality, hanging it with precision, exact spaces between items. No wonder he could not see the crinkle in my lips, or hear the dance in my voice. A tone had been set. Work to be done, no time for niceties or frivolity. The *armada* impenetrable to the outside, to an outsider.

The stoniness of the 'commander', in stark contrast to the raucousness of his crew on their first conquest within the albergue, the tiny kitchen in which I was frying eggs to have with my simple supper. The incursion began. Action everywhere, each member of the detachment in position, armed with a pot, pan, or spatula. I beat a hasty retreat to the outside courtyard to eat my bread, eggs and *papas fritas* in the breezy dying of the day. Rather the solitary chill, than the heat of the production-cum-firing line.

A slow sip of the boiling coffee in the warm cocoon of A Lua, heavenly against the remembering of the previous evening's courtyard. I stretched back in the white chair, my legs extended along the blonde wooden floor. What the hell, I snapped off a corner of a pig's ear, felt its tiny sugary eyes winking against my tongue. A sweet contrast to the mouthful of dark roasted coffee. So much more satisfying than my previous night's dessert, the *jogur melacoton*, that I usually relish every smooth swallow of, but which last night did not, as I had perched uncomfortably, on a high stool, feet dangling, surrounded on all sides, and underfoot by the *armada's* supplies. Uncomfortable, but better than outside in the darkened courtyard, with the wind nagging at my bare legs and frayed mood. The kitchen then, bearable, deserted, but for the mountain of pots and pans left scattered across every inch of stove top and sink.

I had wondered where the *armada* had decamped to for its dinner. I'd followed the sound being funnelled into the kitchen, to determine its location. A door with a sign declared: '*Comidor*'. A passage and stairs down, that until then, I hadn't known existed. But of course, it made perfect sense that the *armada* would find this underground bunker. At least then, the *armada* confined and not conquering.

The meal done, the dormitory was the next to be fully colonised. My top bunk in a far corner, a tiny speck of independence, but so small and insignificant, as to be totally irrelevant. The 'commander' and his crew, busily, noisily preparing for the next day's incursions. Planning, strategising, logistics being put in order. 10pm. Lights out. The rule ignored, the lights still blazed bright.

Against this ongoing dominating power and presence, I had prepared to go to ground. Ear plugs in, buff periscope-like on my head, eye patches over the periscope. Please God it all would help to dull the decibels, muffle the machine. But my defensive measures were no match for the wilfulness and mindlessness of the mighty. An uncomfortable constriction across my forehead. Sweat in my eye sockets. Surrender was my only option. Morning must eventually come.

5h30. Rat-a-tat-tat. The alarm fired. Five minutes later, another round fired off. The crew were now on notice. Lights on. What the hell! The *armada* had simply imposed its way on the entire territory. The entitlement of the coloniser.

My fingers closed a little firmer around my pen, a tightness in my jaw and stomach as, four hours later, I relived this injustice. Pen down, I uncurled my shoulders, up and back, opened my chest.

Australian accents floated above me. A mother and daughter were trying to fathom A Lua's breakfast menu, an actual menu not just a blackboard. Too many choices. I did some basic translation to assist their ordering.

"*Alguno mas*?" Your light, lyrical tones Luz, asking the older gentleman in the checked shirt if he'd like anything else, as your busy fingers folded in the cardboard squares of the cake box, its contents carefully secured.

"*Nada mas*." Coins clinked into your hand. "*Gracias, hasta mañana*." He left with a smile.

You were out from behind the counter, ready to receive the Australians' order. Quick steps, deft hands, squeezing oranges, frothing milk for the *café con leche*. Delivered. Back to the front counter to hand over a long *pan* and a big sucker to a mother and little girl with a pink bow in her hair. Your hands free, they moved to the display basket, a *napolitana* retrieved and plated. Two slices of bread thickly cut and put under the grill, before your momentary disappearance and perfectly timed return, with a soft omelette ready to partner with the seductive smelling *tostadas*. The Australians sorted, stilled. A light clatter of crockery as your hands submerged into the small sink. Hands so active, hands serving, rather than conquering.

My pen and thoughts drifted back to my early morning, to the *armada's* withdrawal from the albergue and my collapse into a few hours of post-battle slumber. The sounding of my alarm at quarter past seven, birdsong by comparison to the 5h30 gunfire. Quiet, dark. No sign of 'commander' or crew, the *armada* surging forward.

I had survived. I would live to see another day, to walk another mile. But, like gun-smoke, the *armada's* energy still hung heavily in the air. I needed to leave, to breathe, to give my own energy time to resurface, but a process would be required. A process, my instinct and experience said would be helped by both place and pen.

A place that the *pasterleria* A Lua, with your presence, Luz, offered space to be. Where I could begin to breathe, not just into my chest, but into the depths of my belly, into the depths of my disappointment at the quality of the previous evening, into my overwhelming sadness at my night of isolation and 'othering'. Of being a lonely island with no connection, no community, no conversation, to provide the protein for my soul that my eggs brought to my body. To reflect on the extent of my own self-reliance and resourcefulness in being this island. Challenges I had met the previous night, but as I swallowed my final mouthful of coffee, and the last sugary morsels of the second tiny pig's ear, I readily acknowledged, I had not fully conquered, and maybe never would.

I thank you Luz, for providing a place and being of quiet, care, and inclusion, of enabling me to step back onto the path with a little less stress and tension in my body, with a heart and soul slightly freer than the one that, if not colonised, had been held captive for the preceding sixteen hours.

Hasta luego

Sharon

Hello Salceda friends

Friends for only a few short hours, on a single day along The Way, before, during, or after the tiny village of Salceda, but the quality of time and togetherness was enough to call you 'friends'. A tea stop, alongside a stripe of grey tarmac, under a monochrome sky, that brought delightful splashes of colour, conversation, and connection. A brightly-coloured, multi-countried canvas, of Spain, South Africa, and the Philippines, bounded by a soft white Mexican frame of you, Alfredo and Guadalupe. All so unexpected, so welcome, after my night of despair and desolation at the Albergue Ultreia in Arzúa. Sweetness, once more, in sharing steps and stories with pilgrims walking the 100 kilometres between Sàrria and Santiago. Wonder, in the subtle interlacing of walking and watching, of presence and perceiving, of being a pilgrim, and being an observer.

Not for the first time, I was drawn to white clothing, this white, not like that of Muriel's un-pilgrim-like shorts, that first passed me at speed, many Camino days' ago. This, a soft, billowy, long-sleeved white shirt, stationary. A sailing boat's spinnaker on a windless day. A contrast to the white, but with the same softness, a dark wispy beard, and shoulder length brown hair in a loose ponytail. I observed you, who would later become known to me as Alfredo, standing just off the path. Your back to the café-bar overflowing its chairs, tables, pilgrims and noise onto the busy morning path. Your gaze trained through a small square, on a field opposite the café-bar – observing a few large wheels of spikey blonde hay, a couple of lazy cows, and a rusted farm implement, that in a previous life, maybe rolled hay. A scene unremarkable, unworthy of the attention of the pilgrims, intent on their *cafés con leche* and *tostadas* at the bustling café-bar, seemingly oblivious to the overwhelming smell of cow dung. A scene, however, worthy of your camera lens, and your concentration, and you in turn, capturing my curiosity.

Further along the road I found you once again within my frame, Alfredo, and felt the smoothness of the energy, that like the ring of Saturn, surrounded you, and landed gracefully on the objects of your seeing. The 'Wall of Wisdom', with its bright orange and green laminated A4 sheets, each sheet, a drawing, a quotation, or a question. An invitation for pause and thought. We stood a few feet apart, silent, in the company of our own questions and answers, within our own musings. Your camera silent too, asleep against the layered white folds of your shirt.

My eyes and thoughts arrested. A rowing boat tilted menacingly, the stern sinking, the bow skyward. Two occupants. The one at the back trying to plug a hole. "Lucky there's no hole on my side" the word bubble above the head of the figure at the bow.

The wisdom offered here and now in Spain, yet universal, and one that talks so fiercely of South Africa. The people at the back of the boat trying so desperately to plug the holes, the privileged at the front, smug, falsely secure in their assessment of the irrelevance of the leaks. My pause long, heavy. Light footfalls, as you retreated from the wall, then stillness and a subtle, spaced, click, click, click.

Later, green, brown, white. A 'foresty' stretch. Deep green on each side of the brown corridor of Camino path, and in the middle, white. Your white shirt now alongside another. Two sails moving forward, just ahead of me, moving in an ease of energy and connection.

"Me gusta mucho tus camisas blancas." I love your white shirts. *"Muy tranquilo"*. My Spanish questionable, but I sensed you understood what I was saying, the feeling of peacefulness that your shirts brought. Your shirt, Alfredo, and that of the older woman whose shoulder kept quiet counsel with yours, whose dark eyes rested tenderly on my face.

A mere sentence, a momentary connection, but one whose warmth cushioned my steps as I continued along the path, as the leafy green and yielding brown gravel gave way to hard grey asphalt, and the modest strip of village – Salceda, generously anchored at its centre by *Casa Tia Teresa,* a place of long pause for my 'sitting pants'.

The hiss of the machine as it spat its boiling watery breath into the mug.

"No necesita gracias", I lifted the sachet of sugar from the saucer and placed it on the tall countertop, to save it from being dripped on, when I pulled my tea bag out of the mug. No response from you, the burly, bearded Spanish man preparing my tea. We stood in silence, your left hand raised, I assumed to recover the sugar. Your big pointing finger came towards me, and traced a faint line down my cheek, hovered in the air, before coming to rest on your tongue.

"Sweet enough." Your words heavily accented. Maybe it was something you'd done and said over countless cups, but it was still a first for me and you, and laughter skipped its way from my stomach, up through my chest and throat and gurgled out of my mouth.

"Si, por supuesto". Yes of course, although I suspected that the taste on your tongue was more salty than sweet. But I would certainly take "sweet" from you, a somewhat gruff charmer.

I sat *sola* in stillness at the table outside. Content just to be, content still in the glow of the morning moon I had been walking in. My restoration in the *pasteleria A Lua* in Arzúa. Content in the warmth of my fleeting interaction with the white sails. My stillness, a contrast to the activity around me. Two blonde German pilgrims ordering *bocadillos*, some light refuelling. A large table of dark-haired, maybe Asian people, having a three-course lunch. I wondered where they were from, something familiar in their way, but from this soundless distance, no clues of language or accent.

Suddenly next to me, not loud, but crystal clear, an unmistakable South African speaking.

"*Sjoe*, I'm starving. I hope the food's gonna be as good as the book said it is!"

The first 'Saffers' I had encountered in the nearly 300 kilometres I'd walked on this way. I didn't immediately declare myself, simply observed. Two women, freshly showered, a sign of a day's walking completed. Two heads of washed, not quite dry hair. One head – dark blonde curls corralled into a disorderly bun, that spoke to me of a person impatient for lunch. At the opposite pole from the bun, turquoise toenails housed by what might be size 8 or 9 cork sandals. Toenails, a shade or two darker than the turquoise of her companion's hair. Interesting colour I thought, what story might such brightly coloured hair and camo pants be telling? The story of an individual who ventures outside the lines, sets herself slightly apart, that says I'm not your average nearly 60-something? Her story? Or one I was writing her into?

Still I sat undeclared, the observer, feeling their different energies. One, soft-edged circles, the other, zigzags with a spike here and there. The tall dark woman went inside.

"How's your walk going?" My introduction to the turquoise, milder-mooded individual.

"Good thanks", you whom I would soon learn, was called Jan, said, not picking up on my being country kin.

"You are the first South Africans I've come across on this Camino."

Still no linguistic recognition from you, or declaration from me of our shared country mother. More questions and answers, you asked where I was from?

"Joburg." The informal shortening of Johannesburg.

Ping. The conversation now on a different track. Not biographical as one might expect, but a tumble of words and thoughts, that had seemingly travelled many miles in your daypack, Jan. Words and thoughts bursting to be released.

"We're together, but not together" you explained of yourself and your fellow South African, Lizzie.

"I really wanted to walk on my own, but it worked out this way, us coming on the Camino together. I'm loving Spain and the Camino, but she's always complaining about things here, especially about the local people who she says are unfriendly. *Geez*, I wish she'd relax and be more accepting. Her attitude is really getting on my nerves."

My role was simply to listen, to be familiar ears in a foreign land. Lizzie returned, a huff and puff in her stride and tone.

"That man is *bladdy* difficult", bristled Lizzie. Some challenges I gathered with getting the lunch order in. Jan's eyes momentarily met mine in a 'what-was-I-just-telling-you?' look.

"Sometimes it's just different ways of being, different cultures, different ways of saying things", I offered lightly. A brief silence. It's our own interpretations, and more often, our own expectations that chafe and rub and become the blisters we bear. This I know well.

"Sharon's from Joburg." Jan's introduction, as I sat down with my tea at your table.

The burly, bearded Spaniard arrived at the table. In each large hand, a colourful platter of frilly green lettuce, long triangles of pale yellow cheese, twisted grey plaits, separated by large squidgy purple full stops. Two streams of smells trailed past my nose. One, subtle, sweet, the other, pungent, powerful. Quince, anchovies. I grinned at 'Big Beard', a hint of a smile on your lips, Lizzie, perhaps the promise of the platter and the basket of bread.

"Let me take your picture with my two fellow South Africans", I said to you, my new Spanish friend. A similar response to the one I received when I handed you back the sugar. Blankness. Okay I thought, maybe you weren't so keen on the idea. No offence taken.

You two, Jan and Lizzie, set to work on your salads, I sipped my second cuppa, we swapped snippets of stories of our lives on and off the Camino, swapped in the ease and fluidity of a shared history.

Then 'Big Beard', you came shambling back, a black beret angled on your head, in your hands a large crooked stick. You curled yourself around Lizzie's shoulders, rested your bearded chin on her bun and beamed broadly. Now you were ready for the photo!

Once again gurgles of laughter travelled from my insides out. This was further confirmation of a gruff exterior that encased the sweetest charmer.

I left you two 'Saffers' to the satisfaction of your sweet and salty salad, while I stepped closer to satisfying my curiosity about the table of Asian pilgrims now surrounded by plates of hollowed out pink prawn shells, a few random French fries and empty Coke bottles.

"Hello, did you have a good lunch?"

"Yes, yes, we ate too much!"

Again, the feeling of familiarity as I edged towards the table; as I felt a thick sprinkling of fairy dust landing on my face and shoulders, as the smiles and warmth of four adults and three children settled upon me.

"I'd love to know where you're from and how you all fit together?"

"The Philippines, we're family". Two sisters, two husbands, three children between them, walking from Sàrria to Santiago.

The familiarity made perfect sense – in seeing them, in my sensing of their energy and enthusiasm. Filipinos, of course. People for whom I have a strong affection, for their kindness, eagerness to please, and spiritedness. For their undying commitment to karaoke!

"You know the Philippines?" an excitement in the asking.

"A little."

"Sit, sit", plates were cleared into columns, chairs shifted slightly to give more space to the empty one I was invited to take up by your two families. The felt familiarity in action. Filipinos as I know them – welcoming, warm, inclusive.

Another sitting and shared storytelling. Of your travels from the Philippines to the lives you now live in the Netherlands and Australia, of your meeting up in Spain to walk the final 100 kilometres of the *Camino Francés*. Of my travels and experiences in the Philippines, and of the Filipino way of being. Our conversation an easy ebb and flow of journeys, geographies, and observations. I asked if you knew of a Filipino gesture, something offered to me at the end of mediation training I presented on the breath-taking island of Boracay, for officials of the Philippine Department of Labour and Employment. A gesture, where everyone had beaten their hands twice on the table and shouted "BEM BEM". Some kind of appreciation or acknowledgement, I had presumed at the time.

"No", the adults among you laughed, you didn't know this gesture, but you had no difficulty at all believing it to be 100% Filipino!

A few more lines, and a little more laughter, and then the time came for me to bid you farewell.

"Thank-you for your welcome, and for this time spent, and *Buen Camino*", I offered as I stood up, pulling my body a bit taller after the sitting. And your delightful reply, many hands beating twice on the table and a loud "BEM BEM".

It was then two *lekker* tight South African hugs, and a "Cheers" to you, Jan and Lizzie. Your last comment Lizzie, one that took me slightly, but pleasantly, by surprise – not surprise in the words themselves, but in the possibilities that they might allow to percolate in you, and in time perhaps, extend their own invitation to you.

"Sharon, you really will talk to anyone."

"Yes, it's one of the wonders of this way. The people you meet, the conversations you have, the surprises and gifts that they might hold."

A light smile from you Lizzie, and from you, Jan, a knowing nod, and I was off, onward to Pedrouzo, the penultimate stop before Santiago.

But still more deliciousness was to be squeezed from the day. Another convergence with the 'white sails', and this time, a 'many-worded' one. A Mexican mother and son. A son walking with his mother in the place of his father, whose knees wouldn't allow him to walk the 100 kilometres. A mother grateful to her son for stepping into his father's boots. A son grateful for the liminal space these 100 kilometres provided between his withdrawal from studying engineering in Germany, and setting foot onto a new path. The path of his passion, a passion explained by his frequent pauses, the focusing, the framing. Photography.

How beautiful was the time we spent, Alfredo and Guadalupe, sitting snuggly, three abreast on a small makeshift log bench in the middle of nowhere, adjacent to a field of nothingness. Not just to feel the fabric, Guadalupe, of the long white sleeve against my bare arm, but to be in the intimacy of your loving energy.

How beautiful to be in the exploration and sharing of our observations of being an observer off and on the Camino – something Alfredo, you do predominantly through your camera lens, and I do through my coach's curiosity about people and their ways of being. To be the observer of our observers, and to reflect on the riches and risks that being such observers bring. Riches in seeing differently, in the opening of new or different possibilities. But also, the risk of distance, in setting yourself apart, safe, unattached, uncommitted.

How interesting Alfredo, to learn of your eyes' particular fascination with the relationship between pilgrims and the path – between those people who pass through with their boots and backpacks, and the people and places that directly or indirectly host the hundreds of thousands of pilgrims who crisscross Spain every year. A fascination that explained the first time I noticed you, your back to the busy café-bar, your focus on the field opposite, towards the haybales, the rusty farm implement. That explained my later noticing, at the 'Wall of Wisdom', that you didn't take close-up shots of the coloured quotes and questions, but clicked your camera from a distance away, where the cards were just a single beam on a broader horizon.

This relationship between those on and off the path, a subject too, of my own interest and reflection. Relationships, so much part of the path. Necessary, important. Ideally and often, relationships of respect and reciprocity, but also fraught, and easily the subject of negative assumptions, unhelpful expectations, and misunderstandings. A subject very much alive for me during my time at *Casa Tia Teresa*, in the interaction between Lizzie and Big Beard, a relationship between a pilgrim and a person integral to the path.

Alas, it was time to leave the mysteries and musings of my warm Mexican cocoon, to step back onto practical feet. With you, Guadalupe, a fond farewell, held within your white sail, and soft flesh. And to you, Alfredo, my good wishes for the unfolding of your journey beyond Santiago, as I continued onward with mine to Santiago, carrying with me, a deep gratitude for the breadth and depth of these heart-and-soul-filled Salceda connections and conversations.

Wherever this finds you all, I hope it finds you well.

Sharon

Mi *amiga* Paloma

'*Una paloma blanca*', a huge 1975 hit for the George Baker Selection. A song, Paloma, I'm sure you would've had sung to you many a time. A song about a white dove, a song about freedom and hope. And you, Paloma, what hope and peace of mind, did the wings of your kindness seek to bring to me, a complete stranger, and to my extended family.

"Sweetheart, Joni asked if, since you are in Spain and we are in the UK, and you can speak Spanish, you can phone Villa Adria and try to sort out our cancelled booking? If we can't sort it out in the next few hours, we're going to have to try to book something else this morning. We'll be leaving for the airport at 2pm, so there really isn't a lot of time."

An early morning voice message from Dearly Beloved as I made my way out of a heavily slumbering and somewhat spitty Santiago. The same city

I had entered about sixteen hours before, but now entirely different in its being. On my early afternoon arrival, a city fully awake and flooded by an enormous tide of incoming pilgrims. Noisy, jubilant, the streets teeming. An afternoon that gave way to an evening of loud pilgrim voices, particularly those of an Irishman, a Dane, and Spaniard, each trying desperately to out 'mansplain' the other in the close confines of the albergue's veranda. Voices more penetrating, more difficult to tune out, because of English being the common tongue. Voices that pounded against my skin and psyche, even after I carried myself and my longed for pasta dinner to a table further away, in the hope of lessening the volume that was dulling the aroma of the onions, taking away from the taste of the mushrooms, peppers, and cheese.

An evening of low-grade irritable itching, that gave way to a night of full blown, literal, scratching. An onslaught of *chincas,* crawling out of the wall next to my bunk, onto my pillow, and one into the hair at the base of my neck. So brazen they were, that I initially doubted them. However, their fat round bodies and tiny wiggly legs in my headlight, complete confirmation. Creatures, whose personal acquaintance I had first made on my eighth Camino, lucky many would say, to have been spared this meeting for so many years. Creatures I had been so careful to never feel directly between my fingertips, as I squashed the life out of them, revenge, albeit unsatisfying, for blood they'd sucked out of me, and the red Orion's Belt of bites they'd left behind. Always many layers of tissue, or paper, between me and them. Now though, in the early hours, in my angry, stinging desperation, and *gatvol* with the frequency and intimacy of this year's 'acquaintances', I ruthlessly clamped one thumbnail against another, the bloated bedbug oozing blood, my blood, out from between them.

How grateful I was, after that night of torment by creatures big and small, to step out of the albergue, and into the cool, quiet, calm of the morning. A morning, however, that was now not just about me and my journey, but one that carried a responsibility in trying to help resolve the problem with the coming night's accommodation at the Villa Adria in Marbella. A problem that until now, Beloved, despite her best efforts and terrier tenacity had been unable to resolve. Their clock ticked quickly, loudly.

"I'll see what I can do. I can't promise success, but I'll try my best." My simple 7am response to Beloved's plea.

And certainly, I would try to help. I was flattered by Joni's faith in my linguistic competence, but highly doubtful that my constipated Spanish would be sufficient to handle the resuscitation of the cancelled reservation due to a confusingly rejected credit card payment. A resuscitation that was necessary to bring peace of mind to Beloved, her daughter, and son-in-law, that they and the two children would have a room when they arrived at 11pm that night in Malaga. A room at the Villa Adria, a room long booked for just a night, before a move to five secured nights at a resort further along the Costa del Sol.

7am, too early take any action, so there was time to zip the task into the top pocket of my backpack and begin a new part of my journey, the 87 kilometre path to Finisterre. A path of deep significance, of long stages, and an abundance of weather! A path I had last walked eight year's ago, as part of my second Camino and Beloved's last Camino.

The kilometres beyond Santiago, so completely different in tone and traffic. A mere trickle of people and packs. So unlike the surging tide, washing a sea of pilgrims down the steep hill from Monte do Gozo, along the wide dual carriage approach roads, and through the snaking streets of the old city, depositing them in a foaming pool on the Praza do Obradoiro, in front of the cathedral in Santiago. The path beyond – soundless, serene, where brick and tar begin to give way to spaciousness, breath, and birdsong.

I paused, three kilometres out of the city, to soak up the pink and purple hues that ever-so-gently caressed the cathedral's towering spires. Stillness, a silent greeting to Cape Town pilgrim Pamela, an acknowledgement and echoing of her deep love and appreciation for this view, for the beautiful shades and shadows it offers, for the nuances and narratives it honours. I breathed into my belly. The cool, dewy morning air 'kissing better' the sting of my bitten skin.

Ahead of me, a small group of four pilgrims. Two heavy-set mid or late twenties' women with black knee-length lycra shorts, and lightweight rain jackets. Each with thick dark hair in a single braid. Sisters maybe, given their physical similarities? Diagonally behind them, two older men, slightly built, light on their feet. One, the father perhaps. Their voices all low, unobtrusive. My pace a little faster, I closed the gap and passed with a smile and a *"Buen Camino"*. A quiet, almost shy *"Buen Camino"* returned from the women, a louder, but gentle one from the men.

Steps in glorious space and solitude. Two voices, not at great volume, but in the 'new normal' of the low volume, less travelled road, voices that seemed loud, voices that were creeping up from some distance behind me. Women's voices. Maybe it was not the pitch or level that began to prickle, but the unceasing stream of words, from one of them. So, a question to myself,

"Do I try to pick up my pace to increase the distance between us?"

No, because I want to walk and not rush.

"Do I just stop and wait for them to pass?"

No, because they were not walking that much faster than me, it could take time for them to catch up and to create a gap between us. Also, I was enjoying the flow of my feet and didn't really want to interrupt it, not yet.

How is it that one person has so much to say? Feels no need for silence or even spaces between speaking? I know my own presence to the path is easily diminished by conversations without pauses, without freedom from speech. That the spaces between, are integral to my way and wellbeing. Possibly, that is just me.

Eventually, or what felt like it, the voice touched the hairs on the back of my neck. Thankfully, not with quite the same impact as the bloodthirsty *chinca*. The voice stopped. Footsteps, the only sound.

"Buen Camino" boomed out.

The greeting immersed me, with the force of a perfectly formed wave breaking on the shallow sand of Beacon Island beach. I gulped in some air, steadied myself, as I looked into the laughing hazel eyes. I smiled, despite myself, it was hard not to, in the face of such enthusiasm, energy, and wholeheartedness.

"*Buen Camino*", my return, positively sedate by comparison.

Now a step ahead of me, I got to examine the voices' containers. My focus was more on the one, probably because she was the one of the 'dominant discourse', the one who had been taking up more space in my world. Brown hair, its bobbed frizz as enthusiastic as her greeting. Turquoise lycra shorts extending into deeply tanned athletic calves, not young, but firm. A bright orange, quick-drying T-shirt met golden toned biceps. An athlete. A mature marathon runner perhaps, who also spends time in the gym. A person for whom I suspect, exercise is a source of happiness, and not heaviness. A person like me! A person whose pace is not that much faster than mine, but whose fleet-footedness, made my body feel heavier, a slightly less well-oiled machine. Yet in truth, I am carrying probably eight or nine kilograms more on my back, and many more kilometres in my legs. And, I sensed this might have been her first day on the path. Not a comparison, or a competition, or a justification, simply a noticing, and an appreciation, that as in life, on the Camino too, everything is relative.

I was however grateful for the women's pace, as it gradually allowed them to pull ahead of me, and I eagerly awaited the return to silence, the sounds of the path, the 'beats in the bar' of my boots. Equally, I awaited a café-bar and breakfast, an uncertain wait, since I had no guidebook or route information, just a knowing that a café-bar would eventually come. A café-bar that I hoped, would bring not just breakfast, but the possibility of help with the situation of the Villa Adria, and the execution of the plan I had devised.

My plan. To seek assistance of a Spanish person, someone to whom I could explain *el problema* of the cancelled reservation and the pressing need to resuscitate it. A Spanish person, who could speak and hear what my Spanish did not allow, and whose status as a native might elicit a different response or commitment, who might less readily be discounted than a foreigner. A Spanish person whose identity was not yet known. Potentially one of the three 'mansplainers' from the previous night? Preferably, the Spanish one in the trio, whose voice delivered itself in just one shape and form. Authority. A delivery that grated on my nerves the previous night, but certainly would be of value to me in the here and now. The voice I will have no surprise to later learn, was indeed the voice of a CEO!

It was 12 or 14 kilometres of walking until I came upon white tables, white chairs, and umbrellas. A Camino oasis. In grateful possession of my coffee and *napolitana,* I plonked myself down at an outside table, where an emerging sun provided the warmth that the swing of my limbs did while in motion. I scanned the tables for who might be my helper. No sign of 'his master's voice'. Murphy's Law!

My project took me somewhat out of presence to my much-anticipated coffee. I finished the cup before I even knew it, or properly tasted it. I headed back to the bar to get hot water for my second cup, scanned the slightly darkened interior, looking for my target. Away from the bar counter, unnoticed, during my first round of coffee, a table of six. 2+2+2. The two younger women and the two older men I passed, and the two women who passed me. All now grouped together over their coffees and juices. A jovial bunch, clearly enjoying the morning and their being together. My eye was drawn to the orange T-shirt, not just to its brightness, but to the energy its occupant was emitting, as she swallowed the last mouthfuls of her *zumo naranja,* stood up and readied herself to leave. Smiling, talking. Of course, she was talking. It was she, the cheerful chatterer!

A last scan of the café-bar, it was now after 11 am and the problem-solving sand was slipping through the hourglass. Time and options were running out. I approached the table.

"*Hola a todos.*" I smiled and greeted everyone. "*Lo siento, se puede aydarme*?" I'm sorry (to disturb), is it possible for someone to help me?

"*Si, si*" six people leaned towards me. An invitation for me to come closer.

I cobbled my Spanish words and sentences together to give the gist of the problem: "If I give the phone number for Villa Adria, could someone please call for me, because all previous attempts have failed?"

"Claro que si".

Movement, as someone sprung forward.

In the Camino's 'stick-its-finger-in-your eye' way, of course the 'springer' was the one of whom I had been, if not outwardly but inwardly critical of, unkind in my 'motormouth' assessment, ungenerous in my assumption that she did not need silence, did not need to hear the path. The same person, who now listened intently to my story, asked questions to check her understanding, explained the problem more fully to her group, and jumped into action. Who, without hesitation phoned Villa Adria, received no reply, left a message, sent text messages and WhatsApps, entered my number in her contact list, and sent me a WhatsApp to ensure our connection. Who promised to keep on trying, and to keep in touch. The person I entered under 'P' in my phone's contact list. Paloma. You, Paloma, who like *una paloma blanca,* would be my person of hope, of possible peace of mind, in the problem of Villa Adria.

And how true you were to your word, Paloma, to keep trying, to keep in touch. I'm not sure what level of perseverance was necessary, how many calls you needed to make. But I do know that when I next checked my phone, there were seven WhatsApp messages from you, a step-by-step setting out, in simple Spanish sentences, of where things were at. The seventh message, the all-important one, that a room for five was indeed secured for that night.

A message that allowed me to walk in greater freedom and lightened responsibility on the path to Alto Da Pena, a day's walk of 47,650 steps. A walk that would provide confirmation to the young Spanish David, my multi-questioning conversation partner, at the Albergue San Miguel in Hospital de Orbigo, that at age 50, I could still walk 30 kilometres in a day. A walk that gave me time, once again to reflect on the gifts of the Camino, gifts that come in different forms. Not just the fierce gift of the 'finger-in-the-eye' and the learning it brings, but the tender gifts this path so frequently offers. The acts of kindness of strangers. Strangers, who through their care, concern, and deeds, cannot be called 'stranger' but must become 'friend', irrespective of whether or not more time is ever spent with them.

And so it was, Paloma, that you became friend to me. Not just you, but your husband and the rest of your group, each one who I could feel holding, not only the hope of your success with Villa Adria, but also somehow holding me in their love and care, on my solo journey to Finisterre.

How happy I was, Paloma, as I set foot into the heavy dripping morning the following day, to see your brown frizz and calves making their way up the thirty stone steps to the bar at Alto da Pena. You, unusually quiet until you saw me, and then a burst of smiles and sentences. Your way of being. A way of being that the previous day's path had invited, or maybe more accurately, challenged to me to become a different observer of. A challenge I reluctantly accepted, but that allowed for different eyes to rest upon you this morning. Appreciative eyes.

It was just you and your husband, the rest of the group walking at a slightly more modest pace behind you. I would see you all together again, be embraced by the warmth of your energy, late the following afternoon, in the seaside village of Cee, as I stood dejectedly a few steps beyond the crisp, white, wonderful looking albergue that had no bed for me.

As I paused to consider my options, the sound of a door closing, the same door that had closed on me moments before. Footsteps, and a childlike squeal of delight. The now familiar voice.

"Sharon, Sharon *estas aqui*!" You are here!

"Y tu quedas ahi?" And you are staying there? As I pointed with envy at the shiny white door.

"*Si, si.* We eat, you come?" Always welcoming, generous, inclusive.

"Gracias, pero no. Necesita encontrar una cama." My priority, to find a bed.

A final *Buen Camino* for your walk to Finisterre and a final thank-you to you, Paloma, for your kindness, for your action, for welcoming me into your heart, and into your walking family. And, welcoming not just me, but my extended family. How wonderfully you breathed and embodied *'Mi familia es tu familia. Tu familia es mi familia.'*

Con una sonrisa, un abrazo y la ultima palabra! With a smile, a hug, and the last word!

Sharon

Querida Lolita

Two 'peas in a pod', and an odd couple. Two adjacent wood and stone benches in the cool, thumping, evening in the coastal town of Cee. This town, unlike its more beautiful Camino sisters, Rabanal, Villafranca del Beirzo, and Molinaseca, is definitively not a case of 'love-at-first-sight', but rather, a friend who with time and without expectation, becomes a lover.

The peas in a pod – two octogenarians, small frames, thinning grey wash-and-set hair, fleshy beige stockings, brown Hush Puppy shoes. Sitting so close, so similar, it was hard to tell where one ended and the other began.

A few feet to the left, but completely unnoticed by them in the intimacy of their connection, the odd couple. A large woman, of similar age to them, but broad shouldered, big boned. A woman of substance and presence, sartorial. Ginger hair in a stylish cut, full bodied, jagged points across her wide forehead. A fine but defined arch of eyebrows, clear brown eyes, strongly announced cheekbones. On each ear, an orange stone set atop a gold plate, a careful complement to the coppery tones of her hair. A freshly applied stripe of rich red lipstick, in striking contrast to the swirling blue and white abstract patterns of her evening dress. Two sizeable white buttons sitting on its generous sloping collar. Proud, unapologetically decorative, rather than functional. A smart padded anorak, beige on the inside, black on the outside, giving further shape and form to this impressive woman.

Next to her, just touching, a woman maybe thirty years her junior, blonde hair, dancing blue eyes. A simple black windbreaker zipped to the neck, a few stripes of blue and black buff peeping out. Camel multi-pocketed quick drying pants, well-worn Salomon boots. Small, sun-browned hands that frequently rose to speech, a constantly appearing toothy grin.

The peas, two unknown 'oldies', decade's long friends. The odd couple, Lolita and Sharon. You and me. Two strangers on a bench on a bustling Sunday evening in Cee. The connection of such surprise, such sweetness. A connection that came, not just in the fading light of a dappled day, but as the sun began to set on my 2019 Camino. A connection that allowed me to touch, and be touched by, the soul of Cee.

Why a dappled day, you might wonder, Lolita? Because the day, as with most Camino days, was not just one thing or another – not one colour, one kind of weather, one mood. But rather, patches of this, spots of that, brightness, and shadow. A day that had begun shrouded in a dense mist, a soggy hangover of the previous 24 hour's incessant rain. A day that had begun in stillness, a respite from the heaven's fiercely blowing breath. A morning that had invited a later than usual start, positively leisurely at 9 am. Why not, when this was the time predicted for the sky to begin drawing back her heavy grey curtain? Why not, since I had made the decision to walk the way from Olveiroa to Finisterre in two stages instead of one? A decision that lightened the weight of my backpack even before I hoisted it on to my grateful shoulders. A decision that brought spaciousness, and ease, to the steps of my now penultimate stage, of this year's path.

Indeed, Mother Earth must have received the memo, and honoured the prediction, because on my 9am departure, a mere 'spit and a spot' that made the green greener, the air so full, you could almost hear it breathing. Tiny drops of moisture held by fine clumps of spindly green thread, blinked against the shy, re-emerging sun. I had started to climb. The path winding gently upward, offering views of a lazy river snaking through the lush landscape below. A pause, as I stood in the embrace of the silence, inhaled the green-scented air. Momentarily, I was not in Galicia, but on a mountain top in the Southern Cape, looking down on the so-called 'Map of Africa', an extraordinary viewpoint at Wilderness Heights that beckons your imagination to see an outline of my continent, its border etched by the dark mysterious water of the Kaaimans River.

I reconnected to the present, gave thanks for the here, and for there, and then continued onward to the village of Hospital. Another Hospital, this one, the last outpost before a long 15 kilometre 'unnourished' stretch between this pinprick of a village, and the seaside town of Cee, my overnight stop.

In the far corner of Hospital's only café-bar, a patch of sun, a sun earlier shy, now grown in strength and confidence. A sun that warmed me on the outside, as my morning coffee deliciously warmed my insides. A sun whose rays were as welcome to the clean, but wet socks and underwear, fastened to my backpack, as the bread, butter, and jam were to my stomach and spirit.

A long lingering in the contentment of the café-bar, and then, onward and upward, onto the high path leading to the wide expanse of mountain top. My company, the solidly standing wind turbines with their whispering 'whirrs'. Long, steep ups. A single cyclist passed by. How grateful I was to be on foot and not on wheels, to be able to look left, right, up, and down, to appreciate the magical pencil-case of colours – yellow, pink, purple, green, brown, blue. The cyclist's only choice, eyes front, as he huffed and puffed his way up the monster hill.

The colours, a dotting of small flowers among juicy succulent leaves. Something familiar about their colour and stature. Low to the ground, but bold, hardy. Survivors against the elements, the whipping winds and chucking rain. In the distance, way above their tiny heads, and the shoulders of the wind turbines, the sea. The very same Atlantic Ocean that licks the shores of Cape Point, that sprays her breath on the yellow, pink, and purple flowers of Cape Point Nature Reserve, Scarborough, and Kommetjie. The familiarity, explained, felt.

A warmth worked its way across my chest, along my arms that stretched involuntarily outwards, leaving my walking poles dangling from my wrists. I inhaled deeply, hoping to catch a whiff of the sea, but no, just the faint aroma of hay and cow dung, the sea still too far away to be smelled.

An added sweetness to the remembering, to the sweetness of that moment, the bright yellow packet I unzipped from the waist-pocket of my backpack. "Life is juicy", the bold red print across it. Maynard's fruit pastilles that had travelled nearly five weeks with me across Spain. One of two packets, a gift from my very dear friend Michelle. The other packet, long given, and eaten by Dearly Beloved on our road trip two weeks before the start of my Camino. My packet, well-hidden, and well carried, now ripe and ready for this moment.

"Life is juicy, indeed!" I said as I skipped a few steps along the puddled path, to the quizzical look of a big brown cow. Oh, the gloriousness of the day, the walk, the moment.

The path began its steep descent into Cee, and a slow deflating in the buoyancy of my mood. Was it the change in the 'outer', that the natural beauty of the high road had given way to an ugly factory, a 'mobile music blaring' pilgrim, and the drab grey outskirts of Cee? Or was it the more subtle shifting of the 'inner', the ever-decreasing number of steps to my physical destination and the inevitable sadness this brings? The following day, being my last day of walking.

A nice looking albergue. Shiny, white wood frontage, the encouraging green *Trip Advisor* sticker fully occupying a small pane on the front door.

"That looks great", I thought, as I moved closer, raising my hand to ring the bell.

Large black caps on a laminated page, *COMPLETO*. I stepped away as if slapped, no point in knocking on the door that was clearly closed to me. My mood, like the barometer in the entrance hall of my growing up home, dropped one or two bars – the difference being, that dropping under the tap of my father's fingertip was a 'good dropping', accompanied by him saying "the South Easter's dying down". Mine, not the good of a low pressure and an easing of the menacing wind.

The door opened and closed. Footsteps and voices. A brief spike as I heard excited tones. Paloma, so happy to see me and I her. An invitation to lunch, but no thanks, the town was full and getting fuller, my priority, to find a bed.

A bed then found in an unnaturally soundless albergue. The *hospitalera* speaking in hushed, heavily accented French tones, explained the minutiae, the myriad of do's and don'ts. Explained from a place of care and concern, but these innumerable whispered explanations, adding to the albergue's *funeria* atmosphere. Not even the 'comfort' of the rustling of pilgrim packets. The three 'mansplaining' pilgrims, unusually not speaking, snoozing on their bunks.

The silence oppressive, I did not shower, but quickly stepped out, in the hope of finding some life, some liveliness on this Sunday afternoon. But the 'siesta streets' were deserted, a depression gnawed at Cee's edges, at my edges. The brightness of the coloured seaside houses muted by the large grey space between me and them. The concrete children's play area and promenade uninhabited. A desultory squawk from a disinterested seagull.

Where was the soul of Cee? I certainly could not feel it, could not feel much at all.

In my yearning to feel, I took off my boots, felt the crunch of the brown, shelly sand, as it scratched lightly at my clammy 'office feet', feet tender and rarely 'un-shoed'. I made my way across the long beach to the water's edge and waded knee deep into the flat, shallow water, flexed my toes in a few silent scales.

Not a pretty beach, but one, like the rest of Cee, that said "take me as I am". A beach that on closer inspection, offered hundreds of tiny conch shells. Collecting up a handful, I felt the lightness of their touch against the palm of my hands, arranged them into a path on the sand in front of me. An attempt to bring some significance to my being on this bland beach, to inject some energy into the wet blanket of a mood that was holding me captive.

Boots back on, I tramped my way back towards the albergue.

Duuf, duuf, duuf, duuf. Duuf, duuf, duuf, duuf. A sudden thumping interruption to the sleeping Cee, not music, but a deafening pulse. The sound throbbing out of a funfair grinding into life. The sound, all the louder in the emptiness of the funfair. Giant bulging eyes of an inflated jumping castle stared down on me and the trickle of townsfolk making their way towards the fair. The smell of hot oil and sugary dough seeped into the air. A lone family at the *churros* stand. Its first customers, ready to collect their packets of deep-fried chocolate-dipped starfish-like legs. I smiled at the little girl standing with outstretched hands. A glimmer of lightness in my flatness, she didn't notice me, her focus entirely trained on the coming treat.

A couple of hours and two-and-a-bit bowls of simple but delicious pasta later, it was once again time to *dar una vuelta,* to take a walk, maybe stop for a cup or glass of something somewhere.

What a different Cee greeted me, oozing life and limb on every side. A queue at the *churros* counter, the bulging eyes of the inflatable characters, now fully occupied with the children jumping excitedly at their feet. People, prams, pounding music. I walked on to the *plaza,* a possible place to pause with my pen. My eye drawn to a row of benches along the one side of the square. Two old women on the one, and one alone, on the other. To sit on a bench, on the side of the square, or alongside a street, a pastime 'oh so Spanish', especially for those of advancing years. How much this aspect of the Spanish way of being appeals to me. Time to sit, to connect, to simply be.

"Why not?" I asked myself. Why not sit down beside she-who-sits-alone, and be with her in this way, or as much as my foreign way might permit? But let me not impose myself, let me first seek permission.

"Puedo sentarme?"

I gestured to the bench. The slightest nod of your head, and so it had begun. A truly blessed time. You and me, Lolita on the bench, in the life and soul of an 8pm Cee.

I don't remember much of what we talked about, nothing significant, the sharing of some basic information, simple sentences that my Spanish would allow. It wasn't the exchange of words that mattered, but a togetherness of hands, feet, and hearts. Of two people so different, who sat in such easy companionship, who both rolled their eyes and clicked their tongues at the obnoxious teenagers revving their 50CC scooters like they were MotoGP racing bikes, in the street directly in front of us.

Our time together was not long, but as sweet and precious as the *Milkybar Buttons* of my childhood. The white chocolate rounds, each individually wrapped in foil, and snuggly stacked in their cardboard tube. A round to be savoured, to be sucked, until its centre gave way. Buttons, of which I was so strongly reminded by the two big white ones on your smart going-out dress. You Lolita, my own 80-something sweet *Milkybar Button*, on a bench in Cee.

My final question to you as I prepared to head on and leave the space on the bench for your friend who would soon be arriving.

"Hacemos una selfie?"

This was maybe pushing it I thought, a selfie with this stranger. You didn't answer in words, but edged ever so slightly closer, sat a little more upright and stared ahead. The picture taken. We looked at it. You, regal, the faintest curling at the sides of your mouth. Me, totally toothy!

A final *gracias* and goodbye.

And so, I left you, in a very different mood from the one into which I had descended on the long downhill into the town, the one that had closed in around me as the afternoon slid slowly, silently into evening.

Around the corner, I ventured into a small sweet shop, and then found a table at a bursting café-bar. The cups, saucers, glasses, and plates, cleared away, I unpacked the contents of my Iceland packet next to the generous cup of coffee. My notebook, precious fountain pen, and my purchase from the sweet shop, not a tube of *Milkybar Buttons*, but a *KitKat* to have a break with.

With a warm glow in my heart, I once again asked myself – what is it about this country that speaks so deeply to my soul, that gives me such joy, joy in sitting *sola* but *tussen die mense*, alone but among the people, not 'my people' but so at home among them? A question that I did not answer, but simply sat in, with a tear that travelled slowly down my cheek, not as a trespasser, but as a perfectly welcome guest.

Thank-you Lolita, for taking me to that place, to that question once more. For sharing your space, for sharing your self, and for sitting with me in the soul of Cee.

Hasta luego

Sharon

My dearest Jens

9 August, day three of my Camino. The entrance into the small village of Cirauqui, sparse, brown, breezy. The narrow gravel track winds its way into a wider cracked concrete path. To the left, a square of hill, steep-sided, flat-topped. A church sitting on its centre, like an elaborate decoration on a handcrafted cake. Advancing up the short, sharp hill, off the waymarked path, a walker that caught my eye. Not the even arm-swinging, almost mechanical walk of a typical pilgrim, but hands held together, under a black backpack. Not taking a straight line, but rather a series of slow, zigzagging strides, at each turn, the slightest pause. Something distinctly contemplative in the stepping, a deep immersion in something else. A pilgrim, yes, but a person walking a little differently on the path, who maybe walks a little differently in the world. A person I suspected, to be walking in a great many questions.

"That's Jens, he'll be going to explore the church." My curiosity obvious, the knowing explanation offered by Jeanne from Kentucky who I had been walking with. "Have you met him?"

"No, I haven't."

I had not known if my response would've been more correct as a "no" or a "not yet". But I had known that if I was meant to meet him I would, and if so, when and where I was supposed to. Quite simply, because this is the way of the Camino, nothing ever a coincidence.

That was my introduction to you, Jens. From a distance, a sighting, not one of your hands clasping one of mine, but your two in a handshake beneath your Deuter backpack.

A brief cameo, later that evening at a table of 'Jays' in the albergue kitchen in Estrella. Jean, Jeanne, James, Jim, and you, Jens. Although your 'J' more of a 'Y'. A lively encounter, especially with two of the group being Irish. I had thought you might've been Scandinavian, both from your name, and your settled, softly spoken way. I had learned two facts about you at that table – that you were German, and that you intended to walk the entire *Camino Francés,* from Saint Jean Pied de Port where you had started, to Santiago. Just two known facts, Jens, but a feeling of who you might be, or at least, who I had felt you might be, as I had observed your 'doing' and 'being'. Clean, neat, in your fresh black T-shirt. Contained. Not one for the limelight, not a place you needed to be, or might necessarily feel comfortable being in. A light gurgling laugh and a playful musicality to your voice. Kind, blue eyes, held gently within the crinkles of forty-something years of smiling.

Three evenings later, I would next see you, feel your stillness and presence as you sat in the largely deserted early evening of a Santo Domingo street, in the dead zone between the tail of the siesta, and the start of *tapas*. You, fresh and clean, a long-stemmed glass of white wine and a bowl of *patatas fritas* on the table in front of you, Irish Jim across from you.

"Would you like to join us for a drink?"

"No thanks", my stomach had said, "time to eat rather than drink."

7.30 the following morning, the same café-bar. The call of coffee and a *napolitana*, for some reason much earlier that morning. I had taken a table next to the door, smiled a greeting at you seated on a silver stool at the tall bar counter. From the TV, perched owl-like in the corner, the distinctively deep tones of Icelandic band, Kaleo. My 'Pavlov's dog' of music, the inevitability of my limbs going rogue at the sound of "Way down we go." Typically, a losing battle to bring them to order.

"*Por favor*" I had pointed at the TV. "*Es posible hacer mas fuerte?*"

A moment's hesitation, a frown that crawled across the bar server's forehead, as he had weighed my request for greater volume. It was a 'yes', "Way down" now two notches up, and I had surrendered to my mutant legs, shoulders and hips. The sweetest surrender, as I had been carried around the small café-bar in the slow, soulful swirls of Kaleo.

Some long stares from the server, not unkind, but with a look that said: "It's not that I don't like it, it's just I don't get it!"

And of you, Jens, my insides laughed as I wondered if your question might have been: "Who is this mad woman, dancing at 7.45 among strangers in the still sleeping Santo Domingo?"

But no, the warmth in your eyes and the smile on your lips, had carried no such question, no judgment, but to my observer, an honouring and a holding. And just possibly, a touch of envy – that 10% of you would have loved to have done that, but 90% would have run in the other direction. You had nodded, you would gladly take a picture for me, so that I could capture the wonder and joy of that moment-in-movement. "Sure", you had said, safely behind, and not in front of the lens.

Another cameo. Another brief being together around the same table. This time, in the unseasonal chill of a 10pm Burgos, at an outside café-bar on a stone plaza under the towering gaze of the cathedral. The rather solemn evening. Australian Clem's last night. The imminent arrival of Jim's brother, and their parish priest, his compulsory companion. Everyone had been tired from the long day's walk and the unending kilometres into the historic centre of the city. Few words had been exchanged between us, Jens, but again a felt sense of your benign presence, as we huddled in against the nasty wind.

It was in the barren beauty of the *meseta*, Jens, that our connection had begun to find colour and form. Not in a great single swathe of speech, one of the Camino ways in which friendship is forged, but rather, at intervals, and in varying degrees of intensity, across this vast brown prairie.

It started with a tiptoe, as the sun had slunk away from the courtyard at the albergue in Hornillos. This time, not a large table of pilgrims, just three of us at the tiny round of tabletop, on the square of smooth fake grass. You, me, and Christina, your equally sweet-tempered German compatriot. How different you two had seemed from me. The two of you so contained, just a tumbler each of *vino tinto* and between you, a bowl of green olives. Me, rapidly turning the tabletop into an expanding canvas of bread and chip crumbs, empty butter wrappers, salt and pepper sachets, shavings of cheese, bisected by rivers of juice of a very ripe tomato. Preparation of my generous supper *bocadillo*. My buttery, busy fingers, intermittently pausing to wrap themselves around the cold can of Mahou. Your hands, Jens, settled in your lap, occasionally rising to lift the scarlet wine to your lips, or to pop an olive into your mouth.

The lightest threads of conversation, talking about our walking. Our words awash in the babbling brook of your laughter. And while our words, like Lego pieces, had begun to sit on top or adjacent to each other, the outline of our relationship was taking shape more from its 'being' than the 'doing'. An ease in our togetherness, a shared appreciation for spaciousness, for Spain, for time-out from the 'other world'.

The next evening, again, a magical being together, and two unique Camino experiences that I would share with you, Jens. One truly serene, the other, totally stomach-knotting.

Castrojeriz, a modest village in the heart of the *meseta*, a village that holds my soul in a way no other village on this pilgrim path does. A village for me, that invites not just a wandering into the place of the soul, but into the territory of the spirit, towards one's spirituality – the place of our deepest connectedness, to significance, to what really matters. Is this invitation extended through the *Hospital del Alma*, the 'Hospital of the Soul', a sanctuary of spirit that the village gives home to, directly at its centre, directly along the path? A sanctuary, but somehow unseen or unstepped into by many pilgrims in their impatience to be done with the *meseta*? Or is it the village's location in the dry, Karoo-like expanse of land, with its wide horizons of brown flatness that offer breath and a stillness of being, that calls one into the furthest reaches of oneself and one's soul?

And in this flatness, two hills – a moderate one that sits directly behind the village and provides a foundation for the mediaeval *castillo,* the other, a mother of a hill, a couple of kilometres beyond it.

It was the small hill with the *castillo,* that had held us in the palms of her hands, as the last traces of the now-softened yellow sun were sucked from the day, and smoothed over by delicate shades of pink and purple. How truly blessed I had felt, Jens, to sit, swallowing deep mouthfuls from the large cans of *San Miguel* you'd brought for our sundowner. To hear the faintest song lines, and to feel on my face, the feathery kisses of the evening breeze. How very beautiful was this 'first', and what a gift to have shared that serenity and stillness with you, a person who in my short knowing, I had experienced as so comfortable in stillness, a person not always in need or want of speech.

But coming down from the sunset, we had indeed talked. Talk that had landed me in deep, deep trouble. It wasn't the subject matter, but the time spent talking and my errors of judgement.

"How about a drink?" your question as we had approached the village square.

The café-bar so enticing, its tables and chairs nestled under vine-wrapped trellises, between long stone flower beds that held seas of purple and green. The smell of lavender and the friendly chatter of the locals beckoning us closer. I had glanced at my watch. 9.30pm.

"Hmm". A pilgrim, ever mindful of 10pm, the 'Camino curfew', the locking of the albergue door. Heaven help those on the wrong side of 10!

But I wasn't staying in a municipal albergue, rather a private one, and maybe this meant a little latitude in the locking. 10:15 or perhaps even 10:30? Rationalised optimism on my part?

"Okay, but just a quick one." Some turbulence in my gut, but also a defiance. Why should an end be imposed on the gloriousness of the evening?

The telling of tales, the passing of time as we had sat in the warmth of the connection. Suddenly, 10:15pm, and despite my rationalising, my optimism, the nibbling in my stomach, had suddenly become a strong churning. Trouble was certainly coming. A quick good night as I had headed for my albergue and you towards your hotel. My heart pounded heavily as I stood at the giant wooden door, closed my hand around the rope-like metal handle. The handle immovable, a mouth pulled tight that sneered, "I told you so!"

No help from the heavens, nor from Jeanne or Christina, or the wiry German woman who had been asleep in the upstairs dorm. All three dead to the world, deaf to the stones I had thrown against the heavy wooden shutters. The tap of the stones no match for the voices bulldozing their way out of the downstairs café-bar. Shit. Shit. Shit.

What to do? Just €3 in my pocket, no way of finding a bed. One source of help. You, Jens. I had found your hotel, your room door, unlike the albergue's, had been open. No explanation required, my presence explanation enough. Yes, of course I could share your room, you had said. No weirdness, absolutely no motive, just simply, a kindness.

First, to an upstairs balcony to make a quick call to Dearly Beloved, to check-in, to say good night. My misjudgement of the locking of the albergue door, nowhere near the complete and utter misjudging of Beloved's reaction to the situation in which I had found myself. So definitely a reaction, and not a response. Mid explanation, the phone had gone dead. *WhatsApp* losing its connection? But no slow beeping, no "Reconnecting to Dee". I tried again. *Nada,* not even a ringing. Again, and again. Nothing.

The penny dropped, a lead sinker plunging to the depths of my stomach. This wasn't a signal gone awry. Beloved had put the phone down on me. Three more attempts, finally a ringing. No hello, just silence.

"Sweetheart, you put the phone down on me".

No confirmation or rebuttal, just five barbed words:

"Get your own fucking room."

No problem, the words on your face, Jens, as I had briefly explained my predicament to you on my return to your room.

"Let's go and find the receptionist, she's a nice woman, I'm sure she can help."

We had found Maria making a late-night cup of tea in the kitchen. Yes, she could give me a room, the price and payment we could settle the next morning.

Eish! How often on the Camino I'd craved staying in a hotel, and now I was, but no savouring sweetness in this stay. Just a few short and horribly fraught hours. And you, Jens, no judgement or opinion, instead quiet acceptance and support.

The next day it was, that we would walk together for the first time – make our way out of the cool morning quiet of Castrojeriz, through the bald brown wheat fields, to the base of the big mama hill. Where, we had begun, not just the stepping into the steepness of the climb, but into the questions and disquiets that we had both been carrying tucked securely into the depths of our backpacks. Questions that would now, on that day, on that climb, find their way into the light of day.

It is sagely said that "when the learner is ready, the teacher arrives". In our case maybe a variation – "when the speaker is ready, the listener arrives", or perhaps more appropriately still, "when the listener is ready, the speaker arrives". I wouldn't presume, Jens, that the questions I had suspected you to be carrying from the first moment I saw you in Cirauqui, were questions you had saved exclusively for my listening. But I do know, that the questions I had carried from afar, and whose answers I so desperately hoped to walk into, were questions only to be spoken when I perceived that they would be fully heard. And it was you, dear Jens, who I'd sensed would be that listener, and who had indeed been that listener, as we made our raw, real, and sweaty way up the incredible incline to Alto Mostalers.

The first few kilometres, you the speaker, and me the listener, and then a seamless handing over of the 'talking piece', as I became the speaker and you the listener. This interaction, so different to the frequent lop-sidedness of my Camino conversations, of my natural bent towards listening and asking questions, of being a container to the breadth and depth of pilgrim outpourings. This, an equal sharing of time, of stories, of the searching of the soul.

The summit reached, and enough having been said, heard, and shared, it was time for me to retreat into solitude and silence, into the processing that follows a dive into deep wells of words and feelings.

"Thank-you for the listening, for the sharing, for the conversation. I'm going to walk on, I'll see you later."

15 kilometres later, to be precise, it would be.

The first ten of these 15 kilometres, tumultuous, outwardly and *en el interior* – the downhill initially so steep, that concrete had been laid to secure both path and pilgrims, and then a more gradual winding descent, back onto the brown parched prairie that stretched as far as my eyes could see. Eyes swimming in salty wetness. Time lapse tears, the after-effect of my questions, brought from the bottom of my backpack, into the brightness of that day.

The next five kilometres, moderating, both in gradient and emotion. No answers to questions, but a decision – a decision that I had not known was waiting for me to make, but one that now having been made, washed warm waves of relief over my body and being. A decision that I couldn't wait to share with you, and that I shared with you and Kentucky Jeanne, as soon as you had arrived in the garden at the brightly muraled albergue in Boadilla del Camino, where I was drinking tea and eating lemon cake, a celebration of sorts.

"I'm not going back to Saint Jean, I am carrying on, continuing on this way towards León."

My decision, not to follow the plan I'd made for the last few days of my Camino, to stop these steps and travel to the very start of the *Camino Francés*, to Saint Jean Pied de Port in the French Pyrenees. There to meet my 'Camino sister', Tara from Utah, and her brother, and to walk with them to Pamplona, to end where I had begun nearly three weeks before. But I'd walked into the knowing that I couldn't go back, I had to continue, to be with the people who were giving my troubled heart a home. To be with you, Jens, with Jeanne, Christina, and our precious Swiss Steffi. A change of plan that had counted against Tara, but who I knew, would understand completely.

How happy you had been when I had told you. Not a loud happiness, but a broad smile and the delightful crinkle around your eyes.

And so, Jens, we had stepped along the way, more deeply into our stories and into our friendship, until a few days later, it had been time to say goodbye. León. The end of my Camino, and the closing chapter of yours. How special it had been, to sit in our small pilgrim circle in the tall shadow of León's exquisite cathedral. To reflect on our journeys – how we'd started, who we'd started as, who we were becoming, how we were leaving or carrying on to Santiago. An evening of such poignancy, a perfect ending. The evening of 24 August 2017. My eighth Camino, your first, the year of our meeting.

Two years of travel together had followed. No yellow arrows or stone waymarkers to guide our way, no coffees, *vinos* or *cervesas* drunk at sunrise, sunset, or under a vacillating Spanish sky. But wonderful wanderings together, and separately, along our paths, supported by *WhatsApp* and *Messenger.* Always a joy to be in the musicality, lightness, and laughter of your voice, Jens. A voice that somehow carried laughter even when you weren't laughing. To be together in our musings and meanderings, held together by a beautiful plait of connection and care, no matter the spaces or distance between our speaking and listening, between the asking and answering of our questions.

A particularly crazy question, one I had asked you in August 2018:

"Are you doing anything on 17 September, Jens? If not, do you want to meet for dinner in Rome?"

"I'd love to Sharonita". Sharonita, the person I had now become to you, a diminutive as soft as a baby's blanket, that I held against my skin. "That sounds so good, but I'll be walking then".

Your second Camino, my first year in eight, of not walking the Camino. At least one of us would be taking some Spanish steps.

So, August 2019, Jens, and the blessing of our being together, once more in Spain. A very short period of physical togetherness, a mere five hours out of a two and a half week overlap of our Camino time. Our starts, both from León, but five days apart, making it uncertain whether we would ever be in sync. Synchronisation at the 'eleventh hour', on the eve of my leaving. A meeting of not just hearts, but hands, and feet, and hugs, a few short steps from the entrance into the historic centre of Santiago. A meeting that required a marathon days' walk for you, from Arzúa to Santiago. Not just gratitude to you my friend for your considerable effort, but RESPECT!

In contrast to the enormity of your final day's distance, mine a modest 22 kilometres on foot, before a greater distance by bus. A day easy in steps, but uneasy in mood. The last day of walking, always a difficult one, a seesaw of feelings and emotions. And how much more so, the ending of this day. Not a day like that in the August of 2017, a day that held the serenity and spaciousness of the walk into León, and the beauty and closure of our circle. This day, this year, one of acute peaks and troughs.

A day that had in fact started in serenity and spaciousness, in the glowing pinks and purples of a pre-dawn Cee. An intensity of colour and quiet, the only sound my heavy breath, and the light breathing of the trees, as I climbed the steep hill from the ocean's edge to the high path above. Steps that became lighter, yet fuller, with my growing gratitude for the moment, for the generously green, yet sparsely populated path, for everything that had been given to me on this year's Camino, for the sacredness of the walk from Santiago to Finisterre.

From on high, faintly visible in the distance, the cliffs of Finisterre. A view that brought a tingling excitement about reaching the iconic *faro*, the lighthouse at the 'end of the earth', and the 0.0 kilometre Camino waymarker. But first, a beautiful, breath-filled descent down to the coastline, and onto the wide white expanse of the *Playa* Langosteira.

How glorious it was to walk in boots that traced their outlines onto the twinkling sand, to walk under a brilliant blue sky, to have my arms caressed by the sun's warm rays, as the water whispered her secrets into my ears. But alas, the freedom and expanse of the beach's broad back, and giggling tide, had inevitably, to give way to the claustrophobia and commercialisation that is Finisterre town. A place of such significance, but to me, a place that had somehow lost its self, its soul trampled under the feet of the masses, pilgrims and visitors alike, flattened by the heavy wheels of tourist buses. How quickly the numbers, the noise, and the unfriendliness of the woman who grudgingly gave me hot water for a second cup of tea, punctured the peace and contentment that I had been walking in.

Leaving behind my half-drunk second cup of now bitter-tasting tea, I had made my way out of town, and onto the narrow gravel path towards the lighthouse, three kilometres away. The Atlantic to my left, a busy tar road, immediately to my right. My pace fast, in the hope that rapid movement would provide an antidote to the malaise that Finisterre town had poured upon my mood. A hope, that standing at the *'fin de terra'*, some significance might welcome and hold me, as I held my journey in my hands. But no such welcome at all. Instead a maddening crowd – a *Krispy Creme* opening day queue at the 0.0 kilometre waymarker, each person, pilgrim or not, waiting for their 'trophy' photo. Hundreds, ant-like, covering concrete and cliffside, guitaring buskers competing with off-key bagpipes. The beautiful blue of the Atlantic abandoned below, an overwhelming sea of people above.

Off to the side I found a rock, stood alone, felt alone. The significance I'd naïvely hoped for, nowhere to be found. Instead, alienation, disappointment, and an urgency to be away from this place, from its clamour and clatter, away from its jollity. The hoped-for soul-filled ending of my journey was simply not to be, at least not here on the cliffs of Finisterre.

A brisk walk back to the town, and straight to the bus kiosk.

"Please God let there be a seat on the 3pm bus". A bus to take me away from there, away from my overcrowded aloneness, a bus to Santiago. Mercifully yes. A long sigh of relief travelled from my shoulders, brought breath that kneaded the tight ball in my stomach. A huge relief in the knowing that I would soon be leaving, a sweet knowing that I would find you, Jens, somehow, somewhere in Santiago.

Santiago's main bus station, a drab, unsightly, grey structure, but that day, one that brightened my mood. Quickly out and onto even quicker feet, feet eager to get to the old city centre. Feet so hasty and disregarding, that I hadn't paid proper attention to where they were leading me. 15 minutes later, a question:

"Where am I?" Not where I should've been, that I knew.

Another 15 minutes to course correct. A familiar street, one that led to the entrance of the old city. Then two familiar faces. Two young women, one French, one Spanish, two of a threesome with whom I had so gratefully walked the last seven kilometres of a long day, four days before. A fast-flowing stream of words of our ways over the past four days. An immersion that provided warmth against a late afternoon breeze that bit at our knees and bare legs. A connection, all the warmer for it being my first felt connection of the day, a day of ever-increasing isolation.

Then a soft voice from behind.

"Sharonita". The bubbling brook tone as distinct, as delicious as ever. My arms around your neck.

"Jens, Jens, and I can't believe it, there you are! I lost the way from the bus station, ended up who knows where, just found my way back, just came upon my lovely French and Spanish friends."

My words tumbling and jumbling in my childlike excitement.

"Sorry, sorry, let me introduce you...."

Two years on paper, but not a minute in practice. A blue T-shirt now rather than a black one, your hair shorter, still curly but a touch finer, a light grey stubble on your chin. But the same kind, crinkly eyes, and gently embracing energy. The picture of us taken by the French woman, Jens, so telling. Me, looking straight into the camera, a row of white teeth from one ear to the other. You, not looking into the lens, but looking at me, holding me as you always have, wholly, fully, in your attention.

Oh Jens, the absolute joy in this meeting, in being able to walk the last kilometre of our Caminos together into the heart of Santiago. But not before we sat down at the nearest café-bar. An espresso and a glass of white wine for you, and a Coke for me, and between us, the last few of my precious fruit pastilles with their sweet reminder that "Life is juicy".

Later, a drink at the Parador, and an introduction of you to Cate, one of the 'Famous Four', now the only one, the other three having left Santiago. How lovely it was for Cate to meet you, she an American, but now resident in your motherland. How lovely it was for me to introduce you as my very dear friend, to be able to introduce someone like you. I know that sounds like making you about me, and I guess in a way, it was, but only because of who and how you be.

A late dinner, a last supper. A supper of many words and much to tell, but still an ease and spaciousness in the being and telling. In picking up the threads we had first begun to weave in Cirauqui in August 2017, to which, ever since we had been adding strands of different colours and textures, remotely and from afar. And now, as we sat in the tiny stripe of restaurant in Santiago, bringing new weaves of words of the ways we'd walked, and the paths we'd travelled since our last messages.

The questions and musings in which we now found ourselves, quite different to those we had lived, breathed, and sweated, up the 'mother-of-a-*meseta*' hill to Alto Mostalers. Words, curiosities, and questions, we shared between mouthfuls of soft centred rounds of warm white cheese and triangles of yellow, red, and green pepper. The food, exotic by my simple culinary standards, but entirely secondary to our sentences and stories.

11pm, time to say goodbye. No risk of me being late, of being locked out of my albergue, the door of The Last Stamp, where I was staying, having a code and not a key. But 11pm late enough after a long and emotional day, and the prospect of a five am wake-up for my early flight next morning. So, a final few steps we took together through the strangely subdued streets of Santiago. A pause, a last hug, heavy, in the inevitable sadness of our coming separation. Then, me towards my albergue, and you to your hotel, a hotel I would definitely not be visiting!

As in the ending in León in 2017, how deeply blessed I was, Jens, to have you once again in my leaving, in the physical ending of my 2019 Camino. To have been seen, heard, and held, at the end of a difficult day, and the ending of this year's way. An ending that brought the significance and soul that Finisterre did not, or could not, but that together, we could.

For this I thank you, Jens. But more so even, I thank you for a friendship that is so deeply one of seeing, hearing, and holding, irrespective of where, or how, or when, our steps are taken.

With love and warm wishes

Sharonita

Hello dear Camino sisters and brothers

'Pedal assist'. A term associated with electric bicycles or so-called 'e-bikes'. Not a motorised bike, a popular misconception, but a bicycle with a battery, that, when a rider is pedalling can generate power that gives momentum to her or his movement. Assistance to one already in motion. Assistance that brings a different experience and, a different quality of experience, that opens new possibilities of routes to be ridden, and the moods in which they are ridden. Contours and kilometres either unattainable or ground out in 'granny gear', that with 'pedal assist', become manageable for both body and soul.

And on the Camino, an equivalent, the hidden hand against my back and pack, my 'path assist'. For me, not the yellow arrows, conch shells, and tall thumb-like waymarkers with their assorted toppings of stones, flowers, hastily scribbled notes, and abandoned boots. All these undoubtedly supportive in my journey, in guiding my way, giving direction, keeping me on track. But the real emotional, and often spiritual momentum that moves my limbs, enhances my mood, and gives a depth of meaning to my journey, my ultimate 'path-assist', the pilgrims who walk The Way.

Not simply those pilgrims whose steps have been or are taken alongside mine, but all those who have come before me, the known and the unknown, whose boots, blisters, and being have been imprinted in fine, deep lines that crisscross Spain's broad outstretched palm. Pilgrims, who lend significance and soul, who have made my nine walks so much more than the sum of their parts.

Beyond the 'assistance' of the hundreds of thousands of pilgrims held and felt in the collective unconsciousness of the path, the pilgrims of my more personal 'path-assist', the deeply kindred spirits with whom I have shared moments, movement, and meaning across my thousands of Spanish miles, and way yonder. Pilgrims who, like the e-bike's battery attached to its spine, have become part of the internal frame of my trusted blue backpack, who are present in each placement of my feet and walking poles, in each pause for coffee, Coke, or random conversation.

The special members of my 'Camino class' of 2013 – Elke, Pam, Tara, Sarah, and Claire. DJ, my 2014 fellow coach-in-arms, how we laughed on discovering our matching professions and post-shower presentation – beige shorts, black T-shirt, black sandals. Our connection, so brief in time, mere minutes, on the narrow street as we washed out on the joyful tide of the singing nuns of Carrion de los Condes. Our Spanish sharing, just a single square of Lindt 70%, smooth, rich, but deliciously savoured in the six years since, between South Africa, Spain, and Singapore. My two soul connections of 2017's way, Jens and Steffi. The pilgrims of my most strongly felt 'path-assist'.

Steps taken and stories written in the past, but that accompany me – living, breathing, ever-evolving entities along the current journey. Stories and relationships, not static but moving forward, on and off the Camino. In the sharing of memories and milestones, moments of madness, and deep meaning, in the years since our meeting. What ways we have travelled together!

Some of our relationships, born in wordy beginnings – an intense after-dinner conversation in the *Refugio Gaucelmo* in Rabanal del Camino, an almost immediate deep dive into hopes and dreams, into what truly mattered, into the fear of declaring "I do". Others slower, a 'becoming' through stages of development, an initial sparsity of sentences, but a strong kernel of connectedness around which thousands of threads of words, written and spoken, were spun. Over time, over the vast miles between the high mountains of Utah and the *highveld* of Johannesburg. A cocoon that in July of 2014, released a beautiful butterfly on the bridge outside of Logroño, a truly blessed reunion, with you, Tara, my Camino sister.

Other relationships that were lightly cemented through stepping or sitting. Spoken steps down the cruel, knee-knocking descent to El Acebo, and eased the journey into Molinaseca. Sitting in the sublime connection of that day's closing. A table of women sharing supper and stories, and freshly picked berries. Relationships forged in laughter, in respect, and support. In appreciation of Sarah's Italian wholeheartedness, Elke and Pam's Canadian-cum-German warmth, and the unorthodoxy of English Claire's Camino – a Camino done in a very different way on a different schedule, with late starts, a 'couple of wines' for lunch, a tractor ride to mitigate the afternoon's long distance; just a pity, the tractor was heading in the wrong direction, more the pity, the slow discovery of this important fact!

The 'path-assist' of 2017, Jens and Steffi. Steffi, so sweet, soulful, searching. Twenty-four years separating us, but a connection entirely unconcerned with, and unconstrained by age. A connection lived in different ways, at different times, in different places. In Spain that year, in Italy where we have twice since then, walked and deeply talked, and in our every day, each of us never far away. Of steps taken, Steffi, under the intense scrutiny of your searching self, others taken in joy, lightness and release, like those, as we literally skipped side-by-side down the baking August 2017 afternoon path to Bercianos.

The latter, a memory that visited me more than once during this year's way, that brought with it, feet that skipped, a mouth that stretched into a great toothy grin, and a heart that held you close. Equally, the memory of you, Jens, Kentucky Jeanne, German Christina and Eve, and English Chris and I in our magical circle, as the sun crept its close down the spires of Leon's cathedral and on the close of my Camino. Our feet together one last time, before they would find their own ways onward.

What incredible richness your soles and souls have brought, not just to those Caminos we travelled together, but to all my subsequent ones. Extraordinary sweetness, but also the bitter-sweet. Moments in the present where I not only remembered, but also felt the past pressing heavily against my skin. A time in that same place, with one or two or three of you, a place then awash in laughter and love, conversation and connection, a place that, at a later time, without you, quite 'other'. An absence, that would bring with it something on the spectrum from a momentary melancholy to a heart-wrenching ache.

The Camino, always 'both and', never just one or the other, but ultimately, my deep gratitude to you all, for your love and ever-presence, for being the hub of my 'path-assist'.

A deep thank-you to the great many others whom I have not named, but whose names I know, who I still carried as part of this path, whose words and ways have brought colour and contribution, who are embodied and embedded in me, despite not appearing in 'the credits', no matter their supporting, and not leading roles.

And, a broader gratefulness to all those who have come before me, the thousands of 'extras' in the enormous cast that constitutes the Camino de Santiago. I acknowledge and thank you.

Sharon

Dear friends

Traditionally, language has been understood to be the act of speaking, an act in which the speaker conveys a message that describes 'what is'. It is the speaker who is therefore the all-important actor, the one taking 'action in language'. Speakers do not, however, speak into a vacuum, they speak to be heard, to be listened to. If no-one listened, would the speaker still speak? The cynical answer, 'yes', but more realistically, a 'no'. Assuming for a moment, that language is simply about conveying a message, without a listener, to whom would the speaker's message be conveyed? Would there be a reason for the speaker's existence? Is it not ultimately the listener, who provides the *raison d'etre* for the speaking?

Contemporary thinking has recognised the limitations of this understanding, and holds that language cannot be so one-sided, cannot only involve one action or one actor, cannot comprise only the transmittal of information to an entirely passive recipient.

And, within the modern thinking, the rather wonderful ontological notion of speaking and listening being "two sides of the linguistic coin", where according to the supremely skilled and care-filled conductor of the ontological coaching orchestra, Alan Sieler, "listening is the unacknowledged side of the coin". Or, in my words, listening is simply no match for speaking, her far sexier sister. It's not that listening does not exist, isn't there 'doing her thing' – it's just that, like the 'ugly sister', listening has been held in very different regard from speaking. Yet, each is needed for the sake of the other, to give wholeness to the other, a kind of 'linguistic *ubuntu*'. An adaptation of the foundational African philosophy, "I am, because you are", or in my words, 'the speaker is, because the listeners are'.

Call it what you will, speaking and listening are undoubtably in a symbiotic relationship, a relationship of action and reaction. Two walking poles, one in each hand. Poles 'plural', that bring a fluidity and efficiency of movement, rather than a single stick that ultimately favours one side of the body, leaving the other side 'unacknowledged' and uncomfortable.

Just as action happens through speaking, listening too is about action. It is only once the message is conveyed, that the real work begins, the never-ending work of our everyday lives, the work of making meaning of what we have heard. It is not the words themselves that carry colours, smells, tastes, and feelings, but the interpretations we give, that weave words and sentences into living, breathing, blood and bones.

I have, over the course of my letters, made frequent reference to 'speaking' and 'listening', and how on the path, my 'linguistic coin' most frequently lands on the side of me as listener, where I walk many miles in meaning-making. Processing not only the words themselves, but also the moods, feelings and bodies that accompany them. A tongue's tone and tempo, the tightness or slumping of shoulders, the weight with which feet or poles are placed, all part of the package, supporting a fuller picture.

The physical path, however, is just one site of language, a significant site certainly, where language is hard at work, where there is 'action in language', as well as 'language in action'. But listening and speaking on the Camino extend way beyond the viney valleys of the del Beirzo, the windswept hills of Galicia, beyond the wayside café-bars and countless coffees, and past albergue kitchens and bathrooms. The Spanish 'speaking' and 'listening' travels across continents and countries, oceans and seas.

It is in these wide expanses, that my linguistic coin lands on the other side, where I become the speaker, albeit a speaker of a different shape and form. It's not a matter of 'getting my own back' or getting even, but rather, a simple passing of the baton. A passing that offers an invitation to my 'storycatcher', Christina Baldwin's magical and meaning-filled descriptor, to share the stories.

I have walked in and with. For the words and sentences I've heard, to be stirred like onions, celery, carrots, and barley into the soup of my story, ladles of which are then served to those 'listening' to my Camino, 'listening' on Facebook to my written, rather than spoken words. Listening that happens from different countries and different contexts, from those who have walked The Way, or imagined walking The Way, to those many steps removed, but whose imagination is invited to step onto The Way. A wider circle of listeners who, hundreds or thousands of miles from the path, begin making their own meaning of my speaking and stories.

What a gift this listening is, your listening to my pen and posts. Not simply in allowing me to be a speaker, by virtue of your receiving and working with my words, but for the nature of the speaking that your listening enables. A speaking and storytelling that becomes possible where there is a different 'level of language', an 'elevation' in the English. This is not for a second to say that I value less, the conversations with those of foreign tongue, because such conversations indeed bring their own wonder of words and ways. Yet, a speaker and listener having the same 'default dictionary', flings open a window of possibility for the 'what' and the 'how' of the speaking. Language less defined, less about doing, constructions more malleable, subtle, and nuanced, greater meanderings and musings about being.

How grateful I am for the listening that I experienced as being given with full presence, attention, and engagement. Not a listening against the background of a ticking egg timer – the anticipation or actual closing down, on the physical path, of the speaking space, closed by unmindful 'mansplaining' or someone who simply cannot help themselves in going 'one up'. The "yes, but let me tell you about the time when I…"

Despite the distance, the quality of your listening, so felt. Sometimes a comment in response to my words or photos, sometimes not.

"I felt like I was sitting with you at the table, I could feel the evening sun on my face."

Sometimes a quote or a thought offered.

"I thought of you when I saw this, Sharon".

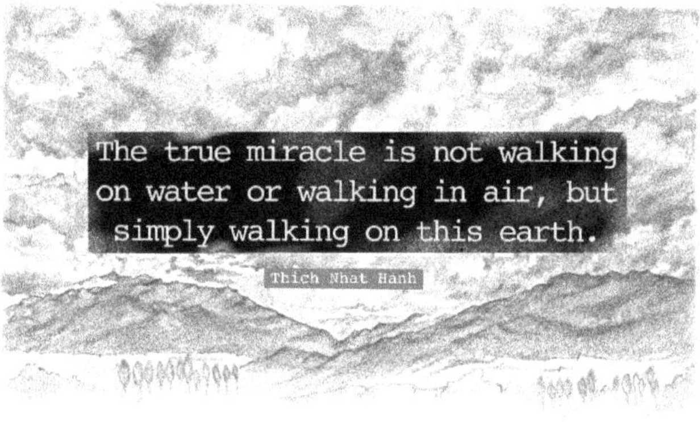

Oh, the magic of this, the joy, words as warming and holding to me, as the morning's first coffee.

To you, my family and friends who have listened to this last Camino, and those that came before, I thank you deeply for the great gift of your listening, for offering yourselves to be part of my daily routine, part of my reflection, for unknowingly travelling with me in my white A4 Iceland packet, neighbours to my notebook and fountain pen.

And beyond me, I thank you for your contribution in giving substance to a significant aspect of the Camino, the sharing of the experience. While I might do the walking, and 'be' the pilgrim, pilgrimage is never owned by a single pilgrim, but carries, and is carried by, the hearts and souls of a great many in unbooted feet.

In words and warmth

Sharon

My darling Dearly Beloved

Each letter preceding this one, has started its way into words, through an assortment of bullet points, thoughts, and unformed sentences. No sequence or syntax, just the random scratches of a gel pen's fine point dotted about on the faint grey Irish lines of my A5 notebook. This one however, has been birthed in a different way. No bullets or brainstorming, but the nib of my fountain pen, aimed directly at the blue lines of my A4 college exercise book. Why not, I thought, just slip straight into sentenced streams, into the mystery of where the ink might flow? Be led by hand and heart across the clean white pages, let my head tag along, be a passenger. So, as you may read from a mood of curiosity, sweetheart, so too do I write. And how delicious is that!

And what if we begin at the end, rather than at the beginning, where I find me and you, most immediately, in our story of the Camino? A starting sentence that says, not only what a great gift your contribution has been, but what a profound joy your companionship has brought me along this worded way. Beyond the keenness of your editorial eye, and the rigour of your reading, the deep wells of love and support that you have offered to each page, to each paragraph, of this writing project.

For me, the '*churros* moment' in the life of each letter, the moment the hot crispy starfish-like leg, just dipped into the rich, thick chocolate, meets lips and tongue, that first taste, and the anticipation of the delectable mouthfuls to come – this moment of the letter, the moment, or rather minutes you would sit, fully occupying the teal corner chair of my office, your eyes closed, head resting gently on the high edge of the chair behind you. Me ready to read, you ready to receive. Oh, the sublime sweetness, me about to be dunked into the decadent dark chocolate, a dunking that would come with the knowing and feeling that I was speaking so fully into the heart of your listening. Thank-you, sweetheart, for this delicious dunking. I'm not sure that you can ever know the delight that tap-danced lightly over my skin, and the comfort of your strong hands that gently held my heart, as I read each letter into your complete listening.

I also don't know if you could ever fully appreciate the anchor that you bring to my adventures, that you have brought to my thousands of Spanish steps. Steps taken in a far-off land, but the way in which I take them, the mood which I take them from, so heavily influenced by where and how in me I find myself; and this is not just about me, but equally about you, about us. It's about having you 'there' when I am 'here'. Not a 'there' necessarily meaning you being at home, but simply in a place that isn't with me, but is there for me, the place from which I feel your 'always' hand on my back. About you being my person, the person who gets me so completely, who knows why I'm having a hard time with X or Y, who understands why I had to leave the café-bar where the guy was working his way through a giant bag of sunflower seeds, shelling each one between his teeth. Why I would have to get up and out, no matter how much I was enjoying the place itself. Why a particular interaction nourished or nurtured me the way it did, or why some absences were so hard to bear. Why I'd choose to walk a shorter or longer distance, to create space between myself and pilgrims whose words or way I did not enjoy, but also, at times, to create space between myself and those with whom I experienced connection, care, and kindredness.

And within this anchoring, sweetheart, some irony, some sacrifice. The time that my time on the Camino, takes away from our time, whether it's time that we could be together at home, or time spent side-by-side exploring other lands and seas. This certainly, a site of struggle in our earlier Camino years, once it became clear that the Camino wasn't your thing – that there were far preferred ways you'd choose to spend your time as a traveller – not day in and day out, to toil heavily across 20 kilometres of Spanish soil, carrying a laden backpack, to arrive exhausted and achy, to sleep on a bunk among the snoring masses, to be constantly at war with your backpack, fighting to find and get things out on arriving at the albergue, and fighting even harder to get them back in the morning after. Vicious contests as arms and legs would do battle with belongings, scorching strings of expletives, but ultimately, inevitably, defeat. You, on one side of the room, your pack and possessions in a disconsolate pile on the other, me, a United Nations Blue Helmet, in the middle, trying to keep the peace.

But my role, more mopping up operation, than peacekeeping mission – assembling your stuff, soothing your mood.

"No more albergue dorms" you had declared.

"Okay, only private rooms or *pensiones*" I had agreed, and assigned myself the task of daily backpack duty. Each morning, I would repack your backpack, place the heavier items in mine, try to lighten the load that pressed uncomfortably on your years-unhappy lower back, that caused your right hip to complain, your knee to shout, your big toe to scream – a scream that I could not hear, but was so obvious from your 'limpy-dog' gait, as you crossed the old stone bridge into Zubiri, after the long, tormenting descent. A slightly lighter pack, *pensiones*, and lesser daily distances, that had made the path slightly more manageable for mind and body, and relationship.

Yet, within the struggle of steps in the pieces of the *Camino Francés* we walked between Saint Jean Pied de Port and Pamplona, and then from

Villafranca del Beirzo to Santiago, so many magical moments of 'us'. Moments that were delicately placed in the 'small blue velvet box', a box that opens, not to release wind-up music, and a pirouetting ballerina, but a box that takes into its most careful safekeeping, moments of intense connection to heart and meaning, where a depth of feeling, emotion, and sensation are felt in each pore and fibre of my being. This box, my 'memory box' where these moments are held.

And, from June 2010, so many treasured memories placed between the fine sheets of mauve tissue paper. Dinner at the entirely unprepossessing Café Fronton, in the 'single file' village of Burgette, near the foot of the French Pyrenees. A simple, but generous dinner of fried eggs, chips, bread, and salad, eaten to the loud intermittent popping of the rubber ball against the players' wooden bats and the high green walls of the *fronton* court. Dinner washed down by a bottle of the local *rioja,* a little rough, but with a nicely smoothing effect, especially under the attentive hand of the owner, ever topping up our tumblers. An owner who undoubtedly had taken a shine to you, and who had so clearly demonstrated this shine – his broad beaming grin, his finger pointing at his wedding band and then, the same finger directed at you, his smile wider still, while his wife had narrowed and rolled her eyes from the other end of the bar counter. Well fed, well 'watered', and with warm wellbeing, our rosy cheeks and entwined fingers had taken leave of the café.

Alongside it in the box, the warmth and the wonderfulness of our connection with Albert and Chus, two true gentleman, decades-long friends with whom we had begun to develop a beautiful friendship along the path. And beyond the path, into their homes, and the homes of their hearts, and their families who had opened their hearts and homes to us in Barcelona and Andorra, the following year. Friendships, sweetheart, so clearly made from the space of 'us'.

Another one for the blue velvet box, not our arrival at the noise-filled Praza do Obradoiro, or rubbing shoulders with the silent spires of the Santiago cathedral, despite their welcome after a gruelling day's walk, but the time spent later that night at a *fiesta,* a few square feet of *fiesta,* at a small square where the larger Santiago meets the historic centre of the city. A chilly wind had whipped around the square and up the street, but zipped up behind our K-Way jackets, doing what we so love to do, dance – together and *tussen die mense*, together and 'among the people' in this significant city, at the end of our first Camino. What warmth and wonder! So definitely moments destined for the velvety inside of the memory box.

How deeply grateful I am, sweetheart, for this to have been my introduction to a path that would become so integral to my being. The *Camino Francés*, the path that we had stepped quietly onto together in a remote French village, as the 2010 World Cup kicked off to a deafening *vuvuzela* start in Johannesburg. A path that we stepped onto a second time in 2011, this time, the *Camino Finisterre* – a walk from Santiago to Finisterre and on to Muxia. Paths that formed the foundation of a far greater journey.

At 120 kilometres, the *Camino Finisterre*, is a short route, but a tough one. And how much more so for you that July, coming freshly squeezed from your sedentary doctoral research week in the vicious grip of a Grahamstown winter. Meeting me, with two weeks of the *Via de la Plata* in my legs, ready and raring for the onward journey to Finisterre. The picture of you arriving in Santiago, stepping off the airport bus, eyes tired but sparkly at seeing my toothy grin. This picture, so different to one twelve hours later, with you, standing at the side of the deserted, early morning park. A thin smile thick with anxiety, knuckles tight around the rubber tops of your walking poles, knees clamped uncomfortably together – a reaction against the crispness of morning, or to limit their knocking, and your mounting fear of what lay ahead?

A fear not unjustified by the challenges of this route – arduous daily distances, grinding uphills under weeping grey skies, guidebook-promised café-bars that provided hope in the long in-betweens, but devastatingly, no longer there.

And, always an 'and', an array of cherished moments, minutes and hours for the memory box. Dipping our toes into the cool massaging waters beyond the wide purple and green 'book-ended' weir, in the picturesque village of Aguapesada, half a day's walk out of Santiago. A late lunch picnic just off the path, in the slow stares of three solid brown cows, and the winks of hundreds of tiny black-eyed yellow and white field flowers. How good the thick sliced Emmental cheese and red-ripe salt 'n peppered tomato had tasted on the generous soft-centred baguette. Each mouthful a submergence into smell, taste, and touch, while being warmed by the eventually present sun. Wonderful minutes of simple pleasure and ease-filled partnership, nourishment of body and soul.

Then onwards to Olveiroa, and the spoil of dinner, bed, and breakfast at the Pension Rustica As Pias. A beautiful stone-walled room, gently infused with the lavender that kissed the neatly rolled towels at the bottom of the abundantly pillowed double bed. A brief departure from the usual bunk or twin beds and quick-drying towels. The room especially welcome, after we had separated on arrival in the village, to survey accommodation options, and somehow had managed to lose each other, despite the modest square metreage of the village. A losing, that, at the end of what had for me, already been an over 30 kilometre day, brought unwanted extra walking minutes and a grumpy mood. A mood soothed by the smell of lavender and the prospect of being enveloped by a large, soft towel, and by a *Menu Peregrino* in a somewhat different league. Food distinctly discernible, different to the 'could-be-chicken-could-be-pork-could-be-fish', of most pilgrim menu's *plato segundo*.

How special were our final steps to reach the *faro* at Finisterre, to stand, with wide smiles, and a hand each placed gently on the 0.0 kilometre waymarker, as if placed lovingly on the shoulder of a dear friend. Then, to have sat together on the cliff, away from the noise of people and place. To have breathed deeply into the thick Atlantic air, to have accepted the invitation that this place, this *fin de terra* so intrinsically offers. The invitation to pause and reflect on that which is being stepped away from, and that stepped towards. To have conducted our ceremony. A ceremony of closing and opening, in which we had acknowledged and honoured the journey, and each other, and shared our handwritten lists of what we were choosing to leave behind. Tore our notes into tiny pieces, tucked them away, and then with spacious hands and hearts, had spoken of what we wanted to carry with us, way beyond the shores of Finisterre.

An invitation, that alone, years later, in August 2019, I either simply couldn't hear or didn't have the heart to accept, amongst the ant-like masses covering every surface of this sacred place. But in July 2011, with you, an immersion into that time and tide, an immersion so naturally destined for the blue velvet box.

And beside it, in the same layer of fine tissue paper, our two-night apartment in Finisterre town, bargained for in a back street in broken Spanish. Low expectations, so delightfully exceeded by the view of the old fishing harbour and across to the lively plaza, a 'safe-in-sound' distance away. A fully equipped kitchen that had opened horizons of culinary possibility after a week of pilgrim menu imposition, and a day that hadn't involved packing things in, or checking ourselves out, but simply, gloriously, 10 kilometres of slow steps, and aromatic sips around the edges of Finisterre.

What of our serendipitous and remarkable encounter on the path between Finisterre and Muxia, with two South African pilgrims, a mother and a daughter? Serendipitous, that walking in opposite directions, we should have crossed paths, or more accurately coffee cups, when and where we did – at the one café-bar in the midway village of that long, less travelled stage. How amazed we had been to see the one litre bottle of olive oil the mother produced from her backpack, to dress their bread and tomato. Amazement for you, sweetheart, that someone would carry this weight, and amazement for me, in the distinct possibility of a greasy pack and oily possessions. Yet, more amazing, the discovery that the daughter's godmother was the dear friend of a dear friend, whom we had met just a month before, at a 50th birthday celebration in Cape Town. And, the 'remarkable' way beyond the *aceite de oliva* the mother was carrying, was that inspired by this journey, she would subsequently carry to full term and become proud mother to the 'Cape Camino'. A generous handful for the memory box, memories as *lekker* as the coffee, conversation, and Cape Town connection, in the middle of 'nowhere-ness' that is the village of Lires, on a random July 2011 afternoon.

Much later that evening, us side by side on a stone bench, sitting in silence, the seagulls respectful, squawking in low, hushed tones. A heavy grey sky rolling in from the darkening sea, the melancholy of an ending creeping closer, pressing down on our drooping shoulders. An ending of that Camino, of your Caminos, sweetheart, but still, one for the memory box, holding each other's hand, while our hearts and heaviness were being held in the spaciousness and spirit of mystical Muxia.

What a gift to have had these Camino experiences with you, to carry this precious box in the most inside pocket of my backpack. Nine years later, to be with you, and Albert, and Chus, in delightful reminiscence, as I passed through Hospital de la Condesa on the path between O Cebreiro and Fonfría. In the harshness of the afternoon's blustery Galician breath, to have the memory box crack open and be sprinkled with laughter and lightness – you, me, Albert, and Chus together, Albert on his phone, ending the call, a broad naughty schoolboy grin and loud voice:

"I told my wife I am in hospital with a woman called Delia!"

To have you, once again, with me on a chilly afternoon, the final afternoon of this Camino, to be offered a sweetness from the memory box, a complement to the sweetness of that moment – Jens and I just minutes reunited, sitting at a table, the fruit pastilles between us. A table, on the very same square in which we had danced among the locals at the *fiesta*, that cold Santiago evening, in June 2010. My 2019 glass of Coke might have been empty, but my cup undoubtedly had runneth over.

The lifting of the memory box's lid, not however always a blessing or a lightness, sometimes a burden to bear. As with times with my Camino community, when the 'now' couldn't or didn't hold the same mood or meaning as the 'then'. A remembering of the same place at a different time, a heart then swaddled, now abandoned. The feeling that had accompanied my most recent 'cuppa' in Finisterre, so very different from before. The café-bar, three floors down from our lovely 2011 apartment, where you and I had drunk many contented, companionable cups of coffee, now offered bitter tea – tea soured by the tight scowl of the host, a woman, as parsimonious with her hot water, as with her personal warmth. A mean-spiritedness I'd usually cast aside with a light curse, but in the felt memory of such 'other', a meanness that had transmuted into great sadness. Similarly, sweetheart, this time at the *fin de terra,* on the cliffs at Finisterre, a time devoid of ceremony and significance. Painfulness in the absence, a quick selfie and a hasty retreat.

Gosh, what a way we have travelled in these words. A wonderful way, for me at least, and I hope for you too. And maybe there is something in that, how far we have travelled together on the Camino. The physical distance we have covered alongside each other might have been around 400 kilometres, but 4000 kilometres, the 'real' distance we have travelled together – the mental, emotional and spiritual distance you have been in step with me. 4000 kilometres in which your love and care has embraced and anchored me, got me through the lows, and celebrated in the highs. 4000 kilometres in which I have been in both spoken and silent conversation with you, shared the beauty, the blessing, or the struggle of that moment.

Thank-you for acknowledging the Camino as a place of my soul, for accepting it as something that adds to me, without taking away from you, or from us; for all that you have given of you, for all the compromises you have made, and continue to make along the way, to make The Way what it is for me.

My depth of gratitude to you, sweetheart, for your being my person, for being my partner on this path, and on life's path.

Yours, as you are mine.

Sharon

Dear Sharon

"I don't really know where to begin."

The starting sentence of the first letter, the letter that began this piece of your Camino journey, the written journey. A sentence, penned some months and many thousands of words' ago. A sentence that is equally applicable here, to start this final flow of words of your 2019 Camino. So, I will begin with this:

Mismatched boots and Beowulf.

So many possibilities of which direction to take, of what to offer you in closing, Sharon. I look up to your bookcase and the objects resting on its smooth Oregon-stained surface. A small stone waymarker, no bigger than six centimetres high and four centimetres in breadth and depth, a memento from your third or fourth or fifth Camino, I'm not sure which. The marker's yellow arrow and conch shell pointing left towards a beautiful Tibetan singing bowl, a gift from your Dearly Beloved, that has given space and structure to many stories in many settings. Beyond the bowl, a blue glass Sugar Loaf Mountain, a keepsake given to you by a Brazilian fellow mediator. And behind the bowl, having travelled vastly different distances to take up residence, two giraffes. One comical, one curious. One brown with long speckled legs, large pointy ears and a lightbulb stomach that made it safely all the way from Thailand, the other, from the neighbourhood African craft shop, a mere kilometre away – curious, a brilliant turquoise body dotted with red and yellow target-like circles, big drooping ears, and enormous black eyes, constantly seeking answers to their questions. Between the giraffes, two tall, skinny-legged, distinguished-looking West African gentlemen, standing with pride and presence in their bright patterned ties, knee length coats, and white pith helmets. One gentleman's helmet decidedly worse for wear, its brim chipped on three sides, from his regular overbalancing and accompanying tumbles down the back of the bookcase.

And, in the middle of everything, a pair of thumb-size boots. One, practical brown leather, with a thick black lace; the other, a delicate white weave, on top of a blue sole, and a cream string lace. Not a matching set, but somehow perfectly paired, complementary. Brown and white, light and dark, yin and yang. Not this or that, rather each giving greater substance and significance to the other. Boots of the 'both and'. Boots, that like their bigger brothers and sisters, allow travel on new and well-walked ways, travel in body and being. A pair of boots in their brown and blue, a reflection of that which is so fundamental to the Camino, its unceasing invitations to step powerfully into that within you which is good, and true, and beautiful; and equally, to step into and embrace complexity, and contradiction of the path, of life. Invitations into the 'both and'.

I wonder Sharon, what it was, that your size seven Salomon boots stepped into along this Spanish way? What curiosity you carried in their grey soles? What gave meaning and significance to your journey, whether in its struggle or its joy?

I know you had started your walking way with musings about who you wanted to be, what could be different about this way, from previous ways, who you had moved towards becoming, in the two years of your Spanish absence, and what you would like to give home to, on this time's path?

I sensed your great wondering, not just about where and how your feet might carry you, but also about how your journey might be influenced by an emergent yet significant relationship – a relationship given substance in the physical form of a fountain pen, a pen that triangulated head, heart, and hand. How you fretted about taking this treasured gift with you – what if it got lost or disappeared? Not that you were typically one for losing things, but in this instance, this fear. A question you posed not just to yourself, but to Jenny, who gave you the precious Lamy.

"If that's what happens, that was what was meant to happen", Jen's eyes, mischievous and crinkling.

A positivity and pragmatism, that gave permission, and opened glorious possibility. The pale green pen promptly took up residence at the bottom of your white Iceland packet, held and hugged by the rough brown covers of the two cheap Irish-lined notebooks.

Never would you have imagined how wide the horizons of possibility would extend, amongst and between your starting steps, in the light, glinting spires of León's cathedral, and the ending ones, on the cliffs at Finisterre, overlooking the blue brooding Atlantic. Possibilities that flowed from the invitation your pen offered, an invitation to pause.

Some pauses, noisy, messy immersions into people and place – into the blaring 'surround sound' of the Sunday night in Cee; into the bursting, bustling café-bars on the Saturday evening canal-side Sàrria street, café-bars whose customers gently, generously, extended the web of their connection to include you, sitting *sola*, but not alone. Being threaded into the warm weave of friends and family, who seeped slowly onto the rain soaked Cacabelos square, a thread of connection offered to you from the most surprising source – from the sensual, larger-than-life belly dancer, who gazed down from her bright muraled self, who rested the dark pools of her eyes upon you, upon your frosted beer glass, and flowing hand, and then smiled, a wide smile of welcome, a smile that wove you, a stranger, into the connectedness of that village.

A connectedness that brought warmth to your heart, as a large, cold, swallow of beer made its slow, savoured way from your mouth to your stomach. And, as if on cue, in that moment of connection and contentment, the smiling face of the waitress, her pointing at your pen in hand and her words:

"Tambien escribo con la mano iquierda."

Two strangers. Two left-handers, and in that moment, two laughs and two hearts that were as one.

Other pauses. Quieter, stiller, more spacious. The corner table, with your tea on the terrace, in Rabanal del Camino; the glorious square of sunlit table, in the serenity of a *Santibáñez* Sunday morning, serenity before the sermon thundered through the slow rising *pueblo*. Pauses of tranquillity and restoration. The Portomarín evening, alone at a then-closed café-bar, held by the warmth of the evening sun, and the sky's heavy after-the-rain breath. Tranquillity, so needed, after stepping beyond the ranting and raging against the 'Sàrria Pilgrims', the judgment of the Saint Jean starters, handed down to those who walked 'only' 100 kilometres, those adjudged unworthy of being called 'pilgrim'.

Pauses, that brought you joy, and pleasure, and presence. Submergences into the sensation of their settings, into sights, and sounds, and smells. Rich coffee, freshly baked pastries, squeezed oranges. Submergences into sensations on your skin. Smoothness in your veins, grains of gratitude, but equally the scratching of irritation, or annoyance. Scratching always soothed, by the spreading of ink across paper. Pauses of transformation, and peace-making. Pauses that began as one thing, and that ended as another. Pauses that embraced both the brown, and the blue boot.

And beyond these horizons, beyond the words written on Spanish soil, in the small brown notebook and iPhone Notes, broad new landscapes of language that beckoned. Two months after ending the physical journey, words, and sentences, that began a flow in a different form. The unexpected emergence of a whole other journey, a new journey that carried the existing journey, that gave a different frame to that experience, to that which had already been written and spoken, as well as that un-worded. A re-remembering, a re-storying, another opportunity to be with people and in places, without the consciousness of needing to step back onto the path, do washing, cook dinner, or be on the right side of the 10pm locking of the albergue door. Being, that could take more of its own sweet time, go broader, and deeper.

Christina Baldwin, the wise-worded woman of Whidbey Island, and person so profoundly of your heart and soul said:

"You'll learn more about your characters in the process of writing about them, understand more about their ways and their being".

How true you found this to be, Sharon, how much more you learned about the people to whom you wrote. Discoveries and deepening. Insights, and enticing avenues for the expression of your imagination. And, always an 'and', a process, that pulsed with intensity, and frequently carried with it, a plunge into wintery waters, into the discomfort of the original time and place. But, as you resurfaced, caught your breath, a new call, to swim towards, rather than splash hastily away from, to observe with distanced eyes, and a slightly more spacious heart, to observe with an openness to make a different meaning. Calls you accepted or didn't. Both and. Brown boot, blue boot.

To move towards a different musing. You had wondered about how this Camino might be different to your previous paths, how you might be different in it, especially given a year un-walked. 2018, the first year in nine, that you had not taken any Spanish steps. Certainly, this 2019 edition seemed for you, far less 'peopled' than previous ones, fewer conversations and connections along the path, fewer people that you will stay in contact with, connections held by a much lighter weave than the substantial strands woven between you and your 'Class of 2013', and between you and your soul brother and sister of 2017.

Despite, or because of the space this absence created, a greater presence to other aspects, to people alongside, or off the pilgrim path. Evening strolls through village life, past gnomes and knickknacks, football fields, and *fiestas*. Street-side sitting on a stray plastic chair. Spaciousness, slowness, and presence, that allowed connection through attunement to that which surrounded you, that gave you a 'home'. Connection also, to what you gave home to, light airy rooms of joy and gratitude, small thatch-shadowed rooms of irritations and disappointments. And, with this presence and connection, opportunities to reflect and process, to make sense of the moods and emotions in which you tap-danced, as well as those you bore heavily on your shoulders, chest, and feet.

Because each pilgrim, consciously or not, walks within her or his own 'Beowulf' – inescapably, engages along the path, in combat with both assorted 'common and garden' monsters, and with 'Grendel', their own 'uniquely assigned' scaly, sharp-clawed creature. Unlike the regular monsters that carry the everyday issues faced along life's way, Grendel, breathes form and fire into the bigger and better known themes of our struggles of the self; replays the more entrenched stories that we live in and into, only now on the Camino, stories offered not just in colour, but in high definition, in 3D. Long-held stories, with historical validity, designed to serve and protect, but stories that we increasingly bump up against, get bruised or blistered by. Stories that ultimately limit possibilities for our different seeing and being.

What a great gift the Camino offered you, Sharon, over the 400 kilometres between León and Finisterre, to venture into the caves and marshes of Grendel's territory, to make eye contact with him, stare him down, or simply nod and step silently away.

How you arrived in Santiago, so grateful for the wide spectrum of steps taken, for the differentness of this journey, for the opportunities of engaging with Grendel. The joy of the closing of this chapter with your dear Jens, and a readiness to leave Santiago, to begin your return to South Africa, after nearly five weeks in your deeply-loved Spain. A final night, and an early morning flight. A last night at the appropriately called Last Stamp Albergue, denoting the final imprint onto a Pilgrim Passport. A passport of not much importance to you, but rather, the importance of a final salutation to Santiago, a goodbye, said in a good way. A goodbye you uttered in *vox baja*, in the late-night chill as you passed through the *Plaza Cervantes*, after bidding Jens farewell. Another acknowledgment, and an *adios*, to the sleeping streets of the old city, as you made your way the next morning towards the airport, this time in a taxi, rather than on the airport bus, a mode meant to bring a shorter, smoother passage.

But, in the way of the 'both and' boots and the story of Beowulf, your arrival at the airport, deposited by the taxi, an arrival of agony and anguish – the end of the plastic Ziplock packet in your waist bag, seemingly sliced with a surgeon's precision, the packet now just two sides of clear plastic keeping each other company, the contents no longer there. €400 gone, but absolutely not forgotten.

So what, that you had found your way through three weeks of Grendel's caves and marshes, only to be waved off by the cruel, cunning of Grendel's mother!

Now, to have to find a way to prise your heart, soul, and psyche, loose from the vice grip in which she held them; the grip of 'should haves' and 'could haves', the softest target in your 'old faithful' story. The discombobulation of Finisterre, and the hoped-for ending that wasn't; nothing at all, next to the heart and gut-wrenching disappointment of what was now threatening to become the ending of your Camino; to swallow you there and then, in the bright light of Santiago's airport, into the darkest recesses of Grendel's mother's cave, into her thin, smug laughter and cold beady eyes.

Beyond your crushing despair, questions that crawled on your skin. Had this Camino been too easy, not enough lessons learned, not enough work done on The Way? 'Higher Grade' lessons still to be learned? But, more immediate for you, Sharon, would you wrestle with Grendel's mother in the depths of her cave, attempt to overcome her, or try to find your way towards the entrance of the cave, towards the light, and leave her behind? Fly away with the €3 in your pocket, sad, but not broken, heartsore, but not strangled by self-recrimination, not overtaken by judgements about oversights and omissions, of lapses in vigilance and mindfulness, on that final night in Santiago?

But more than that even, not to let this scalpel-cut slice through the weave and the wonder of 400 kilometres, not to incise and drain away the blessings that had been embodied on this journey? Was there an active choice to be made, like for the boots on your bookcase, what you wanted to step towards, and to step away from?

Yes, the West African gentleman's pith helmet is chipped. Yes, he has fallen backwards to the floor more than once, but with compassion and without judgement, he's picked himself up, to stand tall, proud, and grounded, behind the boots. In the back of his mind, no doubt, the knowledge that he'd likely fall again, but with a deeper knowing that he could pick himself up again, and the recognition that the falling was not the important part, that the getting up again, was.

Knowing you as I do Sharon, I know that this letting go of self-judgement would have been incredibly hard, despite the processing that you would have done at the time, with and without your pen. I wonder, if now, six months later, in the presence of the brown and blue boots, the singing bowl, the stone waymarker, Sugarloaf Mountain, the giraffes, and the West African gentlemen, and led, once more by your precious Lamy, you would feel yourself free, not just of the fierce grip, but of the whispered growls and subtle goading of Grendel's mother?

That you would see that all that happened, was the way it was meant to be, a part not only of your Spanish path, but also a part of your greater journey, the journey of being human. A journey into the depth of heart, soul, spirit, and compassion, a journey that, no matter how hard it seems, I know you to embrace. To embrace with arms as wide open as those with which you stood, on 2 August 2019, in front of the cathedral in León, before you took a single step on the path; the same arms that, on a distanced rock at Finisterre, wrapped tightly across your chest and held to your heart, everything that the path and the journey had been.

With my deepest love and appreciation, in this ending that is not an ending,

Sharon

Beowulf is an old English epic poem, held to be one of the most important works of early Old English literature, written between 975 and 1025. The key characters are Beowulf, Hrothgar (the King of the Danes), Grendel, and of course, Grendel's mother!

AFTERWORD AND ACKNOWLEDGEMENTS

In August 2020, I was due to walk my tenth Camino. Unusually, I had booked my ticket to Europe six months ahead of time, in February 2020. Maybe because of the so-called 'special' on the airfare. It felt good to have been this decisive, to know that my trusty Deuter backpack and Salomon boots would, within a few months, be on their training schedule around the suburbs of Johannesburg; that three or four months thereafter, said pack and boots, would be stepping onto the path of my heart. Only, that was not the way it was going to be. Not for me, and not for the maybe 250,000 other pilgrims, who would no longer be feeling one of the Caminos de Santiago under their feet.

In March 2020, when, much to the indignation of many pilgrims, Covid-19 first began closing Spanish albergues and café-bars, my overwhelming feeling was that the path that had given so much, and was being called upon, with each passing year, to give just a little bit more, had earned a rest, a time to breathe, to be under less feet, to be for herself, and not for the masses. Surely after decades of selfless service, this was only fair? A few months of not just rest and relaxation, but of recuperation and recovery for the road 'more travelled'. Who could begrudge the Camino this?

But as March crept into April and crawled into May, my perhaps naïve interpretation of a term or semester's 'sabbatical' for the Camino, began to unravel, as Covid pulled and stretched the path and pilgrims, into an uncertain future. As the closing of albergues and café-bars was overtaken by the closing of borders and boarding gates, a single, simple certainty: that my tenth Camino would not be happening in the August of 2020, most likely, not in 2020 at all.

When I began this written journey of my 2019 Camino in late 2019, little did I know that my words would carry me along the path for a further six months. And even less could I have foreseen in October 2019, that this journey would need to sustain me until at least mid-2021.

I am therefore especially grateful for what this worded journey has brought, and what I hope it will still bring me over the long absence of my feet from Spanish soil. More than this, however, is the deep well of gratitude for the close on 4000 kilometres that the Camino has so unselfishly given me in nine years of walking. Maybe a 12-month sabbatical was more just and equitable compensation, than a mere three or four months, for the path to be free from 'active duty'. And quite possibly for the path, not simply a sabbatical to be returned from, but a significant reconstruction of her way of being, accompanied by a decidedly different way of doing for pilgrims. As with so much else that at this time in 2020 is afloat in the sea of uncertainty, so is the shape and form of the post Covid-19 Camino, a mystery, we pilgrims are being called upon to surrender to.

What is far less uncertain, as I sit with my pen in my hand, feeling the warm winter Johannesburg sun blanketing my shoulder blades, are the people I am grateful to, the people who have held, encouraged, and edited me and this work into print and picture.

To Christina Baldwin, writer, 'storycatcher', and teacher-of-teachers, and my 'Self-as-Source' sisters of Whidbey Island, who welcomed me, so green, into their words and wisdom; to my dear friend Michelle Edwards, who immersed her whole self in each letter, way before they found their way into a single text; to Sylvia Nilsen, South Africa's 'pilgrim-among-pilgrims' and Camino servant, for her ever sage and sometimes contrary engagement with me along my many Caminos, for sharing her depth of knowledge as a walker and writer, and for her exquisitely crafted Foreword; to Gaby Andrew, and Pamela Dangelmaier, for their heartfelt reading and rich meaning-making of my words and way, reflected in their generous words about this work; to Abigail Sligcher for the soul, skill, and endurance she brought to the sketches; to Tara Winward for her unexpected and unparalleled proof-reading; and of course to Dearly Beloved, Delia Layton, not just for her careful editing, but for being the right Black Diamond walking pole, to my left, along each and every step of this journey, I thank you all. And to you who have ventured onto the path and travelled these written words with me, my heartfelt thanks.

ABOUT THE AUTHOR

Sharon shares her heart and a home, in Johannesburg, South Africa, with Dearly Beloved and eight, 50-cent-piece-sized-feline-paws, four belonging to Charlie, and the other four to Amber.

As on the Camino, off the Camino, conversation is central to Sharon's way of being and doing. To fund her walking habit, Sharon supports individuals and groups to have better conversations with themselves and others, through her practice as a mediator, facilitator, trainer, and coach.

Deep meaning for Sharon, lies in creating spaces and ways of being together, that enable inclusive discussion, connection, and community-building; ways of being that draw on ancient wisdom, and modern approaches, that not only open broad horizons of learning, but also can support people in living with greater meaning and fulfilment. She values being able to walk alongside others in their journeys to be a touch bolder, a shade braver, and a little different, in how they are in the world.

This is Sharon's first 'full length' journey into print.

For more about her work, visit:

www.beingdifferent.co.za

and for more of her words, see:

https://sharonswordsandway.blogspot.com/

Lightning Source UK Ltd.
Milton Keynes UK
UKHW010724101120
373143UK00003B/385